The new format for *Quiet Sp*
prayer life. There is food for r
ment, wide views for perspe
imagination—ways that lead
with God.
ANN PERSSON

Quiet Spaces offers a fresh, creative and flexible way of encountering the Bible and the riches of the Christian tradition. I hope that its inviting format appeals to many seeking nourishment on their spiritual journey.
JOHN PRITCHARD, BISHOP OF OXFORD

Inspiring, informing and practical, and provides plenty of space for people to make use of the scriptures and themes.
MICHAEL MITTON

For anyone seeking to stay in touch with the Spirit and the scriptures, through earthed imagination and inspired meditation, this is an excellent resource.
SIMON REED, COMMUNITY OF AIDAN AND HILDA GUARDIAN

Quiet Spaces gives a variety of options, and there is flexibility built in for people to work and pray with the material in ways that work for them.
IAN ADAMS

Quiet Spaces offers a welcome and imaginative complement to traditional daily Bible notes, with scriptural and other Christian themes to ponder and pray with over periods of two weeks. The flexible format is most helpful, as we can use the reflections in whatever way fits best in our particular lifestyle.
ANGELA ASHWIN

Contents

The Editor writes 5
Sally Smith

Writers in this issue 6

Images of the Holy Spirit: fire and oil   *Lisa Cherrett* 7
1–14 SEPTEMBER

Fruitfulness   *Pamela Evans* 20
15–28 SEPTEMBER

Gerard Manley Hopkins   *Sally Welch* 35
29 SEPTEMBER–12 OCTOBER

The wisdom of God   *Janet Fletcher* 50
13–26 OCTOBER

The message of Jeremiah   *Sally Smith* 63
27 OCTOBER–9 NOVEMBER

The faithfulness of God   *Jean Sims* 75
10–23 NOVEMBER

Facing the challenge   *Dorinda Miller* 89
24 NOVEMBER–7 DECEMBER

Announcing good news   *Anne Noble* 103
8–21 DECEMBER

Forgotten feasts of Christmas   *Liz Hoare* 118
22 DECEMBER–4 JANUARY

As a Child: Change   *Phil Steer* 131

Spotlight: The Scargill Community 135
Phil Stone

Text copyright © BRF 2014
Authors retain copyright in their own work

Published by
The Bible Reading Fellowship
15 The Chambers
Abingdon, OX14 3FE
United Kingdom
Tel: +44 (0)1865 319700
Email: enquiries@brf.org.uk
Website: www.brf.org.uk
BRF is a Registered Charity

ISBN 978 0 85746 099 8
First published 2014
10 9 8 7 6 5 4 3 2 1 0

All rights reserved

Acknowledgments
Unless otherwise stated, scripture quotations taken from The Holy Bible, New International Version Copyright (Anglicised edition) copyright © 1973, 1978, 1984, 2011 by Biblica (formerly International Bible Society). Used by permission of Hodder & Stoughton Publishers, an Hachette UK company. All rights reserved. 'NIV' is a registered trade mark of Biblica (formerly International Bible Society). UK trademark number 1448790.

Scripture quotations taken from The Holy Bible, New International Version, copyright © 1973, 1978, 1984, 1995 by International Bible Society, are used by permission of Hodder & Stoughton, a member of the Hachette Livre UK Group. All rights reserved. 'NIV' is a registered trademark of International Bible Society. UK trademark number 1448790.

Scripture quotations taken from The New Revised Standard Version of the Bible, Anglicised Edition, copyright © 1989, 1995 by the Division of Christian Education of the National Council of the Churches of Christ in the USA, and are used by permission. All rights reserved.

Scripture quotations from *The Message*. Copyright © by Eugene H. Peterson 1993, 1994, 1995. Used by permission of NavPress Publishing Group.

Scripture quotations taken from the 21st Century King James Version®, copyright © 1994. Used by permission of Deuel Enterprises, Inc., Gary, SD 57237. All rights reserved.

Extract from *As a Child* by Phil Steer, published by lulu.com, 2012

Cover photograph: iStockphoto/Thinkstock

Every effort has been made to trace and contact copyright owners for material used in this resource. We apologise for any inadvertent omissions or errors, and would ask those concerned to contact us so that full acknowledgment can be made in the future.

A catalogue record for this book is available from the British Library

Printed by Gutenberg Press, Tarxien, Malta

The Editor writes...

Welcome to *Quiet Spaces*.

One of the joys of being editor of *Quiet Spaces* is hearing how readers have been using the material it contains. Since I took on the role, I have hoped that people would feel able to use the resource in whatever ways suited their situation, and this has been the case. I have heard of one church that was using one of the themes as the basis of their home group meetings for a term. There is one lady who has used it specifically while on holiday, when she felt she had the space and energy to spend time with God. Several readers have said that they are using it with a group of friends, meeting up regularly and sharing prayer times together.

And of course there are countless other individuals using *Quiet Spaces* week by week, many of whom have told us about how God has been blessing their time praying with *Quiet Spaces*.

I know that many readers have particularly appreciated being able to miss a day without a sense of failure or guilt. We are all different, and so some exercises will suit you more than others. As you learn what draws you to God, give yourself permission to focus on those suggestions that aid you in this and maybe miss out some of the others. There may be times when it is appropriate for you to remain with one section outside the suggested dates; if God is leading, the best thing to do is to follow and see where he takes you.

Maybe as activity starts again after the summer, you might like to try something new; pray in a new place or at a new time, make a new commitment to giving time to your relationship with God and enjoying spending time with him, whether that is a short period each day, or longer periods once or twice a week, or occasional days spent somewhere quiet.

As we approach Advent and Christmas, I invite you to focus on what works and hear God's call to you to draw nearer to him.

Sally Smith

Writers in this issue

Lisa Cherrett is BRF's Project Editor and Managing Editor for the Bible reading notes. She sings in a choir, writes haiku when the inspiration strikes, and takes an interest in new forms of church, alternative worship and the relationship between Christianity and contemporary culture.

Pamela Evans enjoys leading Quiet Days, speaking, and seeing men and women become more fully the people God created them to be. Her books include *Shaping the Heart* (BRF, 2011).

Sally Welch is the Spirituality Adviser for the Diocese of Oxford, working also in a church in the centre of the city. She is a writer and lecturer on spirituality, and is particularly interested in pilgrimage and labyrinths. She has made many pilgrimages both in England and Europe.

Janet Fletcher is in Church in Wales ministry in the city of Bangor. She is the author of *Pathway to God* (SPCK, 2006) and a contributor to BRF's *Guidelines* Bible reading notes. She is a spiritual director and enjoys leading sessions and study days on prayer and spirituality as well as Quiet Days and retreats.

Sally Smith enjoys creating spaces that enable encounters with God through leading Quiet Days and creating prayer corners and stations. She has led prayer groups in her local church, works as a spiritual director and writes and produces education materials.

Jean Sims offers spiritual accompaniment and leads Quiet Days, provides prayer spaces and guides retreatants. She is part of the prayer and spirituality group in her diocese and is involved with leading the Finding Direction Through Prayer course and training spiritual directors for the Diocese of Southwell and Nottingham.

Dorinda Miller has been leading Quiet Days and retreats in the UK and overseas, across denominations, for many years. She is currently involved in running Staying in the Vine, a six-week course on prayer and spiritual disciplines, in Nottingham.

Anne Noble grew up on Merseyside and studied geology at Oxford and Toronto. She is a Team Vicar in Nottingham and is married with two grown-up daughters. She still enjoys geology, reflecting on what we can hear and see of God of all time through rocks. In her spare time she loves gardening.

Liz Hoare is tutor in spiritual formation at Wycliffe Hall in Oxford. She teaches discipleship and prayer and has a special interest in spiritual direction. She is married to Toddy, a sculptor, and they have a twelve-year-old son. Liz enjoys baking, the English countryside and looking after her chickens.

1–14 SEPTEMBER

Images of the Holy Spirit: fire and oil

Lisa Cherrett

Fire: the presence of God

In the last issue of *Quiet Spaces*, we thought about the Holy Spirit as being like wind and water—essential for life but also potentially disruptive, always in motion and unpredictable. In this issue, we consider two other, equally dynamic, elements that can give us insights into the nature of the Holy Spirit—fire and oil.

Jesus once said to his disciples, 'I have come to bring fire on the earth, and how I wish it were already kindled!' (Luke 12:49). His wish became a reality at Pentecost, when individual flames of fire appeared over the heads of all his followers gathered in the upper room (Acts 2:3). As the disciples watched (or, perhaps, as they thought about it afterwards), they might have remembered the flaming pillar of fire that guided the Israelites by night across the desert towards the promised land (Exodus 13:21). It was a visible sign of God's presence with them and of his determination to remain with them and lead them on. Fire is mesmerising wherever it is seen, capturing and holding our attention; in a domestic setting, it speaks to us of comfort and security—a warm room and a hot cooked meal.

If you have the opportunity, watch a bonfire, light an open fire in the hearth or stove, or simply light a candle. Keep watching as the flames burn low. In prayer, thank God for the life-enhancing properties of fire—light in the darkness, warmth in the cold and a focal point that attracts our attention and enables us to find our way. The fire of the Holy Spirit is all these things to us, and more.

You may be feeling at the moment that the Holy Spirit's fire in you is burning low. If so, remember that it was said of Jesus, 'A smouldering wick he will not snuff out' (Matthew 12:20, quoting Isaiah 42:3). Pray that he might blow gently on the flame to re-ignite it in your spirit.

Fire: protection against evil

Imagine camping outside in a remote wilderness place where predatory animals roam free. You hear them howling or roaring as they hunt for food. A constantly burning fire would be your first means of defence: it's a deterrent to wild animals, which instinctively understand its dangers. Now imagine a whole city ringed round by a wall of fire: this is the city of God as described in Zechariah 2:5. The fire replaces the stone walls that had been Jerusalem's security until they were destroyed by Judah's enemies at the time of the exile.

If, as Peter puts it, the devil 'prowls around like a roaring lion looking for someone to devour' (1 Peter 5:8), the Holy Spirit within us is like the fire that frightens the lion off and keeps it at bay. We are protected against evil. The language of computing has adopted the same image: a 'firewall' is a security measure that protects the hard drive from being damaged by malicious viruses.

Cut an A4 piece of thin black card or thick paper in half lengthways, and then cut rough flame shapes out of it. Cover the empty spaces with red, yellow and orange tissue paper, foil or cellophane. (Coloured sweet wrappers could be used.) Tape the ends of the strip of card together to create a reminder for yourself of an encircling fire.

You could use this circle of card as an aid to prayer, helping you to focus your thoughts on the protective power of the Holy Spirit as fire.

A consuming fire

Fire brings reassurance, guidance and protection, but we can't escape the fact that fire is also destructive and dangerous. Should we, then, be afraid of the Holy Spirit as fire?

If you have read *The Lion, the Witch and the Wardrobe* by C.S. Lewis, you might remember Susan's question about the lion Aslan: 'Is he—quite safe?' Mr Beaver replies, 'Course he isn't safe. But he's good.' In a similar way, the Spirit is not safe—but he is good.

With this in mind, read and meditate on 1 Corinthians 3:12–15. If we dared to allow the consuming fire of the Holy Spirit to burn inside our hearts, what would be burnt up? Do we, in fact, know the difference between the worthless 'wood, hay or straw' in our lives (which would be consumed) and the precious stones and metals that would survive the fire? Sometimes we ignore attitudes or activities that we know, deep down, to be hindering our relationship with God. Equally, though, we may be too hard on ourselves, perhaps imagining that our ordinary everyday interests, if unrelated to church or traditional ways of serving God, are of no value to him.

The Prayer of Examen is a form of prayer in which we think back on the experiences and emotions of the day and try to recognise where God was in it all—what he was saying, how he was acting, and whether we felt close to him or far away. In a variation on the Prayer of Examen, it might be helpful to ask the Holy Spirit to show you what needs 'burning up' in your life and what would survive any such testing. In 1 Corinthians 13:13,

Paul says that faith, hope and love are three qualities that will 'remain', so we can be assured that any words or actions based on these characteristics will certainly come through the fire like precious stones.

You might like to journal anything that God shows to you during this prayer time.

Purifying fire

Today, leaving aside the thoughts of the worthless things that the Holy Spirit would burn up, we shall think a little more about the precious things left behind. The Holy Spirit is not content simply for these qualities to survive; he wants to go even further and increase their value to him.

Fire is a purifying agent, not just a consuming or destructive force. Malachi 3:2–3 describes God's Spirit as a 'refiner's fire'. In industrial processes even today, furnaces are used to refine precious metals by separating out impurities such as carbon and allowing them to be removed. This process makes the metals less brittle as well as more beautiful.

Think of the stressful, pressurised times in your experience—times when, as we say, 'the heat is on'. Peter says that we should not try to avoid these 'trials'. Instead, we should see them as opportunities to have our faith purified (1 Peter 1:6–7). Similarly, Job (who was no stranger to fiery trials), in a rare moment of optimism about God's dealings with him, says, 'When he has tested me, I shall come forth as gold' (Job 23:10).

Is there one particular trial in your life at the moment that God might want to use to purify and strengthen a quality in you that is precious to him? Instead of trying to escape it, could you allow the Holy Spirit to come into it with you and bring you 'forth as gold'?

To help you to concentrate on the idea of the Holy Spirit as a purifying fire, you could listen to the aria 'But who may abide?' from Handel's *Messiah*, the words of which are based on Malachi 3:2, or you could meditate on pictures of molten metal. If you have access to the internet, search Google Images for some pictures of molten metal or visit www.loupiote.com/photos/26781866.shtml.

The foundry

In the heat of a furnace, metals are melted before being moulded or hammered into shape to make useful objects. These metals are not necessarily the obviously desirable ones such as gold or silver; they could be less glamorous ones, for example, iron or aluminium. Nevertheless, the shaping and moulding process results in items such as tools or household implements that will remain fit for their purpose for many years to come.

Jeremiah was taught a valuable lesson by God as a result of seeing a potter at work (Jeremiah 18:1–10). What could we learn by going to a foundry to watch a metalworker with his fire and moulds?

The aluminium scrap is piled high all around. Its value is high, but in its present state it is shapeless and useless. I run my hand along the cold, hard surfaces. There is such potential here, but how can it be made real?

I feel the unbearable heat before I see the furnace—blindingly bright, with a roar that leaves me in no doubt of its power to annihilate. This is not a safe place to be.

The metal pieces are lifted from their resting places. Do they have to be subjected to the ravenous flames? They are given no choice—they drop and disappear into the overwhelming heat, and we wait.

And here comes the 'melt'—a silvery river, once-solid metal transformed by the fire to a substance that can take whatever shape the foundryman chooses. He brings out the mould prepared for it—prepared in advance, out of sight, and only now brought into view. He pours the molten stream at a precise speed. Too fast, he tells me, and gases will be trapped, weakening the finished object; too slow, and the metal will begin to solidify before filling the mould completely.

The heat is off. The metal cools. The roar of the furnace can no longer be heard. With concentration, the foundryman releases the metal from its mould, revealing a machine part intricately designed for a good purpose, to enhance the lives of many people.

At last, the formless lump on a shelf has become a lovingly designed and crafted object—and the fire and the foundryman's skill have made it happen.

Fire for transformation

Heat is an agent of transformation in some chemical processes. The energy supplied by the fire causes the atoms of two or more substances to react dramatically with one another, perhaps creating a completely new substance. For example, if the metal sodium is heated up and combined with the gas chlorine, they react together to produce salt.

We, too, as we submit ourselves to the fire of the Holy Spirit, receive the energy to be changed. As Paul puts it, we are being transformed 'from one degree of glory to another, for this comes from the Lord, the Spirit' (2 Corinthians 3:18, NRSV).

As we saw earlier in the week, the Holy Spirit as fire is not safe, but the Spirit is good. This fire consumes what is worthless but purifies and transforms what is really valuable to God. To finish our meditations on Holy Spirit as fire, here is a prayer made up of several phrases. Say as much of it as you wish, trusting in the goodness of the dynamic, fiery Spirit.

Lord God of the pillar of flame in the desert: reassure me of your presence and lead me in the ways you choose.
Lord God of the firewall: protect me from the forces of evil and surround me with your love.
Lord God of the consuming fire: burn up everything in my life that has no lasting value in your eyes.
Lord God of the purifying furnace: hold me steady through the trials and pressures of life, and bring me forth as gold.
Lord God the divine foundryman: melt me and mould me into a useful and beautiful form, to serve you well for years to come.
Lord God of blazing glory: transform me into your image and excite me with the promise of the future with you.
Amen

Oil of anointing

We move from the most dangerous to perhaps the gentlest biblical image of the Holy Spirit—oil. Begin by reading Exodus 30:22–33 and 2 Corinthians 1:21–22, which talk about the act of anointing.

In Exodus 30, the objects and people (that is, the priests) involved in the worship of the Lord had special perfumed oil poured over them as a sign that they were dedicated—set apart, or made holy—to the service of God. 2 Corinthians 1 connects 'anointing' with the presence of the Holy Spirit in our hearts. It is a sign that we are owned by God and dedicated to him.

Anointing with oil still plays a part in the British coronation service, in which the monarch dedicates herself or himself to the nation and to God. Anointing is therefore a very solemn act, but this does not mean it's a sad or gloomy one. Psalm 45:7 and Isaiah 61:3 speak of being anointed with 'the oil of joy' or, in some translations, 'the oil of gladness', and the word-pictures being drawn in these passages are of extravagance, beauty and celebration.

In a few minutes of quiet prayer, meditate on 1 Peter 2:9: 'You are a chosen people, a royal priesthood, a holy nation, God's special possession, that you may declare the praises of him who called you out of darkness into his wonderful light.' Place yourself in an 'open' position, perhaps with hands open on your lap, and ask for a new anointing of the oil of the Holy Spirit, to set you apart for whatever joyful purposes he may have in store for you.

If you can obtain some kind of oil (perhaps baby oil, a carrier oil such as grapeseed, or even olive or vegetable oil from the kitchen cupboard), pour a small amount into your open hand. (Do note that you shouldn't place undiluted essential oils directly on to your skin.) Enjoy its smooth, warm quality and then, if you wish, anoint yourself on the forehead with it as you pray.

Prayer perfume

Look back to Exodus 30:32 and 37. Why do you think Moses and the people of Israel were forbidden to use the special perfumed anointing oil and incense in everyday life?

Perhaps it had something to do with the fact that the sense of smell is linked with one of the deepest parts of the brain, which humans share with many other creatures—the part that deals with both emotion and memory. I can still call to mind the smell of the hymn books, covered in sugar paper, that we used for assembly at my primary school. When I remember the aroma of my hymn book, it brings back the whole atmosphere of early mornings at school and the happy anticipation of singing in assembly, from as much as 40 years ago.

Also, however, the sense of smell quickly gets tired: we notice a new scent straight away, but it soon fades. This is why we find that, after a few days of wearing it, we cannot smell our own perfume or aftershave.

So, for the Israelites, the special perfume of the anointing oil and incense would have created an association in their minds between that distinctive aroma and the act of worship. It would have become, over time, a powerful aid to worship, focusing their attention on God. But if used commonly, in everyday life, it would soon have lost its special associations and simply faded into the background.

Although we are no longer expected to worship God solely in 'special' places (see John 4:20–24), you might find it helpful to build up an association between prayer and a particular fragrance. Find a candle with an unusual scent—or, better still, create your own combination of perfumed oils to use in an oil burner. Essential oils can usually be found at your local pharmacy. Keep your special candle or fragrance set aside for use during your times of prayer and see if it enables you to settle more easily into a focus on God.

Oil of unity

Psalm 133:1 says, 'How good and pleasant it is when God's people live together in unity', and verse 2 goes on to describe the anointing oil poured on the high priest Aaron's head and trickling down on to his robes. Notice that this is not a tiny dab of oil on the forehead—it is a generous flow!

Meditate for a while on the connection between oil, unity and priesthood. Oil is a lubricant. It's able to seep into the smallest of gaps between, say, the metal parts of a door hinge or an engine, reducing friction and wear and tear, and enabling those parts to work happily together as one unit, without damaging each other.

A priest is called and anointed as an 'intercessor'—literally, a go-between. He or she 'stands in the gap' (Ezekiel 22:30) between God and humanity, to bring reconciliation. As an intercessor, we too might stand in the gaps, asking God to reconcile individuals, families, colleagues at work or even nations.

The oil of the Holy Spirit, given permission to flow into the gaps between people, reduces friction in relationships, prevents breakdown and enables us to live and work together in 'good and pleasant' running order.

Do you know of a relationship (between other people, or one in which you yourself are involved) that is suffering from friction? Does there seem to be a painful squeaking or crunching noise whenever these people get together? Is breakdown imminent, as in an engine that needs a top-up of oil?

In your time of prayer, ask for the Holy Spirit to come into that relationship as a generous flow of oil, to lubricate the parts and bring the unity and cooperation that are so badly needed.

Oil as fuel

Another use of oil is as a fuel for burning, to give light as well as other forms of energy. In biblical times, of course, oil lamps were commonly used (see the parable in Matthew 25:1–13).

In our own day, oil is an ever more precious energy source, used for transport and manufacturing of all sorts. Wars are fought over access to it, panic sets in among motorists at the first hint that its supply might be threatened, and fears run high about the fact that it will one day run out completely. No such fears are necessary, though, when we think about the Holy Spirit as oil: God's Spirit is a free gift to us (but no less precious for that) and is the ultimate renewable energy source. This is especially good to remember if we recognise that our physical energy is declining over the years, or if we are simply tired at the end of a long and busy day.

Read and try to memorise 2 Corinthians 4:16: 'Therefore we do not lose heart. Though outwardly we are wasting away, yet inwardly we are being renewed day by day.' Let this verse lead you into prayer, thanking God for the renewable oil of the Holy Spirit and asking for the supply to keep on flowing to you and through you.

If you would like a visual image to help you focus on prayer today, try watching a lava lamp—perhaps our closest equivalent to the oil lamp. If you don't have a real one, you can search on www.youtube.com for a video of one.

Oil from crushing

Oil is a beautiful substance, but where does it come from? Oils used for food and fragrance are often extracted from fruits, seeds, nuts and other plant materials by crushing. In industry, crude oil comes from ancient crushed plants and animals, which then have to be boiled at different temperatures to produce gases such as butane, or petrol, or lubricating oils. In other words, the benefits of oil that we enjoy—sustenance, fragrance and energy—are created under painful pressure and trial.

Think for a few minutes about the idea of 'crushing'. Isaiah 53:5 describes a servant of God—thought by Christians to represent Jesus the Messiah—who was 'crushed for our iniquities', as 'an offering for sin' (v. 10). Spend some time in prayer, thanking Jesus for his willingness to undergo this suffering for our benefit, remembering that the result was an outpouring of the Holy Spirit at Pentecost.

Sometimes, too, we ourselves can feel 'crushed in spirit' (Psalm 34:18). If so, we can take encouragement from the picture of the Holy Spirit as oil: the crushing need not be the end of our story but can, in time, produce a new outpouring of the strength we need.

You may find it helpful to give physical expression to the feeling of being crushed by squeezing juice from a fruit such as a lemon or orange. In prayer, you could offer this squeezed juice to God, asking for the Holy Spirit to transform your painful experience into something that will bring sustenance, fragrance and new energy to yourself and other people.

God's grandeur

The opening lines of Gerard Manley Hopkins' poem 'God's grandeur' say:

> *The world is charged with the grandeur of God.*
> *It will flame out, like shining from shook foil;*
> *It gathers to a greatness, like the ooze of oil*
> *Crushed...*

At the end of our meditations on oil as an image of the Holy Spirit, bring your thoughts together in the prayer below, perhaps using your specially scented candle or oil burner as a focus for the senses as you pray. You can pray all of the phrases if you like, or take just one or two, allowing them to lead you into further prayer of your own.

Like the ooze of oil crushed, may your Spirit set me apart and anoint me for glad and joyful purposes.
Like the ooze of oil crushed, may your Spirit be the fragrance of worship to me.
Like the ooze of oil crushed, may your Spirit bring unity and peace into all my relationships.
Like the ooze of oil crushed, may your Spirit keep me burning with renewed energy day by day.
Like the ooze of oil crushed, may your Spirit turn pressure and suffering into healing and strength.
Amen

15–28 SEPTEMBER

Fruitfulness

Pamela Evans

Introduction

With scarcely any time left before his arrest, Jesus chose to teach about bearing fruit, so it must be important. To set the scene for our theme of fruitfulness, read what he said to his disciples (John 15:1–17). Now focus on verses 4–8. For the fruitfulness Jesus had in mind, it seems that a close (joined together) relationship with him is essential. What do you think he meant by 'separated, you can't produce a thing' (v. 5, *The Message*)?

Soil and crops were part of everyday life in Jesus' day, so telling stories about such things would have seemed perfectly normal. However, when Jesus spoke about 'the vine' there was an added dimension: a vine was used as a symbol of Israel (for example, Psalm 80:8–9). I wonder how those listening felt when they heard Jesus referring to himself as 'the *true* vine' and calling them his branches?

If you're a gardener or have other relevant expertise, you'll be well aware of the dynamics of growth and fruitfulness referred to in biblical passages. Readers with little experience of cultivation may enjoy exploring a section or two with a friend whose passion brings the subject alive. Should the opportunity arise for weeding, pruning or compost-spreading together, you could look for parallels in the realm of personal growth and fruit-bearing while tending the garden. Afterwards, it would be good to pray for one another's lives to be fruitful, incorporating images from your garden work into your prayers.

We'll be reflecting on fruitfulness from a variety of angles. If you use a computer regularly, why not change your wallpaper to something representing fruitfulness, as a way of keeping the topic in mind? Is there a house plant or garden project on your 'to do' list? If so, why not reflect further on the readings for these weeks while you attend to it?

Roots

As in the garden or field, so in the spiritual life: the invisible really matters. Our 'roots' in God are unseen but vital! The following affirmation includes themes and images found in scripture (notably Psalm 1:3; Jeremiah 17:7–8; John 15:8). Read it aloud, slowly, several times. Pray that your heart may receive the truths you are hearing. If questions arise, allow God by his Spirit to bring the answers in his own time; try to avoid going into 'thinking mode' to search for them.

An affirmation of life and fruitfulness

God, I trust you, my confidence is in you.
You have given me all I need to be fruitful.
  I have been brought into being by you.
  Rooted in you I find stability. I draw strength from you.
  You nourish me where I am, and I stand tall.

God, I trust you, my confidence is in you.
You have given me all I need to be fruitful.
  When the heat comes, I sweat but I need not fear.
  My roots are safe from all that threatens to overwhelm.
  I lean in to you, and am sustained by your Spirit.

God, I trust you, my confidence is in you.
You have given me all I need to be fruitful.
  When all around is desert parched, I won't shrivel or crack.
  In your mercy, you refresh me: your living water never dries up.
  My well-watered heart stays pliable, ready to respond to you.

God, I trust you, my confidence is in you.
You have given me all I need to be fruitful.
  With a thankful heart I praise your name.
  I contemplate your words of life to me.
  I shall bear fruit that brings you glory.

Composting

In the wood near my home, greenery turns autumn brown. With time, fallen leaves will decay and replenish the soil under the canopy. In my garden, compost heaps provide ideal conditions for decomposition (darkness; moisture and heat—but not too much of these). Grass cuttings and much else that looks like 'waste'—vegetable peelings, cardboard egg boxes and a whole host of other bits and pieces—may be composted. Eventually, these will turn into the sweet-smelling melange beloved of gardeners.

Scripture assures us that 'in all things God works for the good of those who love him, who have been called according to his purpose' (Romans 8:28). I've found composting a helpful picture to use when reflecting on this verse. After one of life's rogue waves had knocked me down, I found myself floundering in the shallows. I became aware that God was at work in the aftermath, bringing understanding and building strength for the future. If I'd majored on self-condemnation—'How feeble! I should have coped better!'—I might have missed the blessings. Father God is ready to 'compost' the fall-out from undesirable experiences into something to nourish us towards maturity. Pride obstructs this work, whereas humility (accepting that we can't breeze along, controlling every outcome) keeps us open to his plans to nurture us towards greater fruitfulness.

Pointers towards prayer

Composting has many parallels with the life of faith, not least that it takes time… If waiting time always feels like wasted time rather than fruitful time, ask God to show you how he has already used it in your life. If you keep a journal, this may yield helpful reminders.

Compost develops more quickly if thick stems are shredded before adding. Is there something painful you'd prefer to bury whole in the garden of your heart, rather than let the Master Gardener help you process it? Ask God to show you if you are keeping a disappointment alive by brooding over it when it could be released for 'composting'.

Things that won't rot down can't be composted in the garden. Likewise, there's no point in hoping that a sin will disintegrate with time. It lives on until dealt with as God has ordained, by confession and repentance. Is there anything you need to bring to God now?

Soil

Although known as the parable of the sower, Jesus' story (Matthew 13:1–9, 18–23) is really about the soils. Visualise the features he describes; then, if you are able, take a walk in a garden, park or other cultivated space. Linger in each area:

path, pond or stream, shrubbery, woodland, rockery, flower bed, whatever there is in your part of the world. Which areas look well-tended? Are plants growing in cracks in the paving or sprouting between rocks? Give God time to speak to your heart through what you are seeing.

Alternatively or in addition, sketch (or diagram) the areas described in Jesus' parable: the well-trodden soil alongside the path, the parts of the field and what has grown in each. The sketching is to help with opening your heart to God; as you draw each one, allow God to illuminate that area of your life. If you have doubts about your artistic ability, consciously lay them aside lest they distract you.

For prayer and reflection

Is your family, work and church life 'fruitful', or would 'choked by worries' feel more apt? Do any of Jesus' descriptions of the conditions hampering fruitfulness (vv. 19–22) apply to your life? If you have sketched the field, why not write or draw your responses in the appropriate section as you bring them before God?

Jesus does not see the hearts of everybody as equally fruitful: even in good soil the yield varies. Have you ever asked him why?

Prayerfully review what has come to mind during this exercise. Is there something you choose to turn away from as not being part of God's plan for you right now, or an insight you'd like to welcome as part of re-dedicating the garden of your heart to him? Thank him for the good seed he has already sown there, and for what has grown or is about to grow as a result.

After resuming everyday activities, expect to receive additional insights. Consider using your sketch of the parable or a verse or two from the passage as a continuing focus for prayer.

Green shoots

In business and in other areas of life, the expression 'green shoots' is used to describe the first indications of better things to come: the good times are some way off, but at least they're coming—or so we hope. So, what are we hoping for right now? Maybe we hope for things of which the green shoots have yet to appear. Is it, perhaps, a matter of 'hope' rather than 'expectation'?

Our focus today is on nourishing hope. Spend a few moments committing the time to God. You may like to pray, 'Jesus, Lord of life, plant and nourish your hope in me.'

Take a sheet of paper and list as many of your hopes as come to mind. Write with your heart, not just your head. Hope in 'the God of hope' (Romans 15:13, NIV) undergirds everything else, but hopes don't have to be overtly spiritual to be worth writing down during this exercise. Ask God to bring to mind any hopes you've squashed or abandoned. If you become aware of fears preventing you from moving forward in hope, make a note so that you can return to them later.

Lay the sheet of paper before Father God. Tell him what's on your heart and listen for his response. You could ask God to show you which hopes he'd like to nourish, and to reveal channels by which such nourishment might be received.

Reflecting on God's character, his love and compassion, his goodness and faithfulness, is one way of nourishing green shoots of hope (see, for example, Lamentations 3:19–24). Another is spending time with those who trust him: brothers and sisters in Christ who will speak grace and truth to us, and offer support as we seek to travel in hope with expectation.

Unlike apricots or cherries, spiritual fruit may appear at any time. If we're totally focused on hopes on the distant horizon, we may overlook fruit that could be providing encouragement en route.

If you feel stuck on a particular hope, bring any frustration to God and take time to listen to his response. Returning to this exercise on another day might allow you to go further in dialogue with God regarding the same hope, or you might find yourself being led down a different route.

Branches

If you've researched your family tree, you'll have a mental picture of branches of offspring linked back to an individual. Some people discover that, centuries earlier, they had a royal ancestor; others find connections they'd prefer not to acknowledge, but if they're connected, they're connected!

We, who are branches of 'the true vine', are both joined to him and connected through him. Paul was picturing a similar organic connectedness when he wrote about the body of Christ (Romans 12:4–5; 1 Corinthians 12:12, 27). Are you aware of being joined not only to Christians you know but also to all those around the world who are 'in Christ'? How do you feel about that?

Reading what Jesus had to say (John 15:1–17), it would seem that his followers have been chosen to bear God-glorifying fruit—'fruit that will last'—*together*. Let's explore a few of the ways in which we may express fruitful connectedness:

Praying for fruit. For example, praying for: teachers, parents and grandparents who minister agape love, grace and truth to children; a person seeking to stand for fair pay, safe working conditions and good relationships on the factory floor or in the board room; people faithfully sharing kindness and gentleness with those unable to care for themselves. It's not just about 'official' ministries: all can be fruitful where they're planted.

Giving time or money to resource the work of others. In some places, small sums of money, well-directed, bring staggering results. Other ministries need brothers and sisters in Christ to give time, as a one-off or regularly.

Sharing encouragement. Letters to missionaries used to take weeks to arrive, and some never did. Today, it takes only a moment to ping an email around the world saying, 'Thinking of you. How may we pray for you?' and to share news of your recent encouragements. Many women and men in challenging situations closer to home value similar messages.

Make a note of the names of those with whom you are connected 'in the vine' whom God seems to be highlighting for your prayers today. You could write your own prayer or use the one below.

Thank you, heavenly Father, for my brothers and sisters in Christ. Thank you that together we may bear fruit that will last and bring you glory.
I pray for [names], asking you to refresh them with your living water, and to increase their vision for the ministry you have assigned to them.
Please show me how you want me to express my connectedness to them today and in the coming days.
Amen

Pruning

> ***Every branch that does bear fruit he prunes so that it will be even more fruitful.***
> JOHN 15:2B

Fruit farmers know that neglecting to prune leads to trouble! Trees may produce nothing but leaves, and may eventually impair the growth of other trees or obstruct the landowner's access.

Visit a park, orchard or tree-lined boulevard and spend time looking at the trees. (If this is not possible, take the walk in your imagination.) Can you spot a tree that has been skilfully shaped? Mature trees may have been cut back repeatedly. What might one of them look like now had it not been cared for in this way?

Find a quiet place and focus on the verse heading this section. Pruning is part of caring for and shaping a tree or plant. Dead and diseased sections are taken away, but so are some that look perfectly healthy, so that the tree or plant may give of its best.

When God 'prunes' us it can feel like punishment, but it's not! Is 'being pruned' part of your experience of God's care? Have you ever ducked out of a pruning session with the Master Gardener? (Often, it's only with hindsight that we see it as 'care'.) Talk to Father God about your thoughts and feelings, and listen out for what he'd like to say. Can you trust him to shape you further, so that you may give of your best, to his glory?

Bearing fruit

Many scholars think that Paul wrote the letter to the Philippians from Rome during the prolonged house arrest mentioned in Acts (28:16). It's a remarkable letter, not least because it shows that he has learned to pray with joy and thankfulness in such circumstances. Chapter 1 covers many topics, but let's focus on what it has to say about fruit. Read it slowly, engaging your heart. Can you sense something of Paul's passion for the gospel, his affection for his brothers and sisters in Christ and his desire to bear fruit for God's kingdom? Once you're familiar with the chapter, reflect on as many of the following sections as time permits:

The **fruit of the Spirit** is 'love, joy, peace, forbearance, kindness, goodness, faithfulness, gentleness and self-control' (Galatians 5:22–23). Notice how many aspects of this fruit are reflected in what Paul has written to the Philippians—and to us. Today, as we yield to 'the Spirit of Jesus Christ' (Philippians 1:19), he enables us to bear this same fruit. Take a moment to thank God that he is at work in your heart in this way, making you more like Jesus.

Review the verses in which Paul mentions fruit:

- the **fruit of righteousness** (vv. 9-11; see also Hebrews 12:11; James 3:17–18): It seems that 'sowing' righteousness may be expected to yield more of the same and to bring glory to God. Where have you seen this principle in action?
- **fruitful labour** (vv. 19–26): while Paul lives, he expects to be fruitful (v. 22). Are you confident that God can enable you to bear fruit in all circumstances to the end of your days? Bring him your hopes and any lingering disappointments.

The gospel has been advanced in unexpected ways during Paul's incarceration (vv. 12–18). If you also are facing challenges, allow the Holy Spirit to minister encouragement as you reflect on Paul's account of fruit borne in adversity. Be honest with Father God about any mixed feelings.

Being fruit

Today, we're celebrating the fruit seen in our daily lives.

Decorated Christmas trees look beautiful, but the baubles are tied on for a few weeks at most. Genuine fruit develops from within and reflects the character of each tree or plant. In the same way, the fruit of our lives reflects our character. Desirable attributes 'tied on' for display purposes may provoke admiration but, if there's no connection with our inner life, contrary habits of thought and action will eventually shake them loose. Jesus said, 'Each tree is recognised by its own fruit... A good man brings good things out of the good stored up in his heart, and the evil man brings evil things out of the evil stored up in his heart. For the mouth speaks what the heart is full of' (Luke 6:44–45).

Paul exhorted the Ephesians (5:8–10) to live as 'children of light'. The 'fruit of the light' includes 'goodness, righteousness and truth'. Elsewhere, Paul offers further examples of 'what pleases the Lord' (v.10; see also 1 Timothy 6:11; 2 Timothy 2:22). Make a list of the attributes Paul mentions, and any others that come to mind. Then commit your day (or, if reading this at night, your sleep and the following day) into Father God's hands. Go forward in faith, not performance anxiety! If possible, carry with you a reminder of our focus—say, an apple, a packet of raisins or a photo that speaks of fruitfulness. Pause briefly when you are able, so that God may highlight, for example, a time when you respond out of kindness to a colleague, family member or stranger, or speak a word that brings shalom peace. If you become aware of having acted out of frustration rather than patience, don't come under condemnation: seek God's forgiveness straight away (1 John 1:9) and anyone else's, if applicable.

Prayer focus

At the end of the day, thank God for the fruit he is growing in you—fruit you have seen and fruit you have yet to see. Are you ready to pray for growth in Christ-like character so that you may become even more fruitful?

Praying for the harvest

Jesus sent people out, saying, 'The harvest is plentiful, but the workers are few. Ask the Lord of the harvest, therefore, to send out workers into his harvest field' (Luke 10:2). Later, Jesus' Great Commission (Matthew 28:18–20) clarified the tasks to be accomplished and the extent of 'the field'. Our roles differ, but all may pray!

Allow the Holy Spirit to lead, as you 'ask' as Jesus instructed. Here are some prompts to prayer:

Look out of the window: pray for more workers to be equipped and called to serve God in the lives of people passing by; in the homes and other places you can see.

Look at a newspaper: pray for areas featured, for seed already sown to be watered and to come to fruition; for God's call to bring in the harvest to be heard.

Look at a world map: choose a continent, then narrow your focus to one particular area. How is the Lord leading you to pray for those in authority there, for his people and their leaders seeking to live out their calling? Pray for men and women from elsewhere who have heeded God's call to work there, and for those whom he is preparing to call—that he will bless them, and prepare their hearts to respond.

Thank the Lord of the harvest for the privilege of sharing in what he's doing in the world. Close by re-reading the scriptures above, allowing the Holy Spirit to highlight particular phrases as prompts to continuing prayer.

Fruitfulness

Harvest celebration

Preparation

Bring together things representing God's bounty: fruit and vegetables, other food, drink, photographs, anything that reminds you of God's provision for your needs.

Reading

After the great flood, the Lord God 'said in his heart... "As long as the earth endures, seedtime and harvest, cold and heat, summer and winter, day and night will never cease"' (Genesis 8:21–22).

A response

> *Praise, O Praise our God and King;*
> *Hymns of adoration sing:*
> *For his mercies still endure*
> *Ever faithful, ever sure.*
> SIR HENRY W. BAKER, 1821–77

Keep silence as you reflect on all that the word 'harvest' represents. Take time to smell the fruit, or call to mind the aroma of ripe fruit and the fragrance of your favourite flowers. Remember the people who bring these and other blessings into your life, including those who prepared the ground so that you might come to faith.

Break the silence with celebrations of God's faithfulness! Thank him for all his good gifts; for his provision for your needs during the years leading up to today—including those in which you were unaware of him or had turned away. If you are able, sing these words:

> *We plough the fields and scatter*
> *The good seed on the land,*
> *But it is fed and watered*
> *By God's almighty hand;*
> *He sends the snow in winter,*
> *The warmth to swell the grain,*
> *The breezes and the sunshine,*
> *And soft refreshing rain.*
>
> *All good gifts around us*
> *Are sent from heaven above;*
> *Then thank the Lord, O thank the Lord,*
> *For all his love.*
>
> MATTHIAS CLAUDIUS, 1740–1815, TRANSLATED BY JANE M. CAMPBELL, 1817–78

Reflections on fruitfulness

When taking time out

Paul prayed that his brothers and sisters in Christ might be 'rooted and grounded in love' (Ephesians 3:17; read vv. 14–21), 'bearing fruit in every good work, growing in the knowledge of God' (Colossians 1:10; read vv. 9–12). Use these scriptures to pray for yourself, for those close to you and for others who come to mind. (My book, *Shaping the Heart: Reflections on spiritual formation and fruitfulness* (BRF, 2011) looks in more detail at the fruit of the Spirit and offers further reflections on fruitfulness.)

In daily life

Listen to *Gardeners' Question Time* (Radio 4, or via www.bbc.co.uk) or a similar programme. Note the participants' desire for their plants to flourish. Marvel at the effort expended in creating the right conditions for horticultural life and fruitfulness. Then reflect on all the Master Gardener has done and is ready to do for you: none of the plants painstakingly nurtured by the gardeners is as highly valued as you are by God.

In the United Kingdom some product labels reveal that the producers have been appointed to supply the royal family. We, too, serve and bear fruit 'By Appointment' (see John 15:16). Use the labels as prompts to remember whom you serve and why.

The righteous… 'will still bear fruit in old age' (Psalm 92:14). Our friend Elsie illustrated that well: when immobile in her later years she continued to pray for many people, including our (then) teenage sons. When visiting someone with a lifetime of experience of following Christ, why not encourage them to share memories of their faith journey? You could then tell them about some of your reflections on fruitfulness and pray together, asking God that you may both be increasingly aware of how best to serve him fruitfully.

29 SEPTEMBER–12 OCTOBER

Gerard Manley Hopkins

Sally Welch

Gerard Manley Hopkins' life and influence

Gerard Manley Hopkins was born in London in 1844, the eldest of nine children, to a family of devout High Church Anglicans. He studied classics at Balliol College, Oxford, and it was while he was a student that he converted to Catholicism, an action that caused distress among his family and friends. He decided to devote all his energies to his faith, and in May 1868, while still a student, he made a bonfire of all the poetry he had written, and stopped writing. In 1870, he became a Jesuit, and began teaching classics at a Jesuit school in Roehampton. Gradually he came to the conclusion that poetry was not incompatible with religion and in 1875 composed *The Wreck of the Deutschland*, a poem commemorating the death in a shipwreck of five nuns who had been fleeing the harsh anti-Catholic laws in Germany. In 1877 he was ordained priest and, after several teaching posts, was made professor of Greek and Latin at University College, Dublin. He died of typhoid in 1889.

Hopkins' influence on poetry writing was considerable; his language was as striking as it was original and his innovative use of rhythm gave even more life to verses that already resonated with metaphors and allusions so that it seems as if the poems themselves will leap off the page and take on a fully three-dimensional shape. Hopkins' devout faith and his great gift for observation are directed towards helping us to see not just God in creation but the visible result of the outpouring of God's love upon his world.

Gerard Manley Hopkins

One of the challenges of accessing the poetry of Hopkins is that his sentence structure and use of unusual vocabulary can be off-putting and has the potential to form a barrier between the reader and the meaning of the poem. It would be a pity if this meant that the poems went unread—better perhaps to try to establish the overall intention of the poem rather than worry over specific words; the flavour of the work will be evident even without recourse to a dictionary or explanatory notes.

Look up Gerard Manley Hopkins' poetry in an anthology or on the internet, and try reading one of his poems out loud, as this can give a dramatic impetus that will overcome hesitations over exact meanings. Reflect on what God may be saying to you through it.

Hurrahing in Harvest

You received without payment; give without payment.
MATTHEW 10:8, NRSV

Hurrahing in Harvest

Summer ends now; barbarous in beauty, the stooks rise
Around; up above, what wind-walks! what lovely
behaviour
Of silk-sack clouds! has wilder, wilful-wavier
Meal-drift moulded ever and melted across skies?

I walk, I lift up heart, eyes,
Down all that glory in the heavens to glean our Saviour;
And, eyes, heart, what looks, what lips yet gave you a
Rapturous love's greeting of realer of rounder replies?

> *And the azurous hung hills are his world-wielding shoulder*
> *Majestic—as a stallion-stalwart, very violet-sweet—*
> *These things, these things were here and but the beholder*
> *Wanting; which two when they once meet,*
> *The heart rears wings bold and bolder*
> *And hurls for him, O half hurls earth for him off under his feet.*

In this poem, Hopkins is rejoicing in the abundance that surrounds us all at harvest time. Both the power, which is as strong and mighty as a stallion, and the delicacy 'violet-sweet' are evident as Hopkins walks in the countryside. These wonderful sights just lack one thing—someone to notice them and, on noticing, to give thanks to the creator for all he has made.

We know that worship should include our whole lives, not just that small proportion of time we spend in church. But more than this, our whole lives should be given to God—our work and our leisure, our creativity and our other gifts. Hopkins devoted his life to witnessing to God's love as demonstrated in the glories of his creation. He used his gift of poetry to help others see the extraordinary in the everyday, beauty in those things which surround us in our ordinary lives. We may not have gifts of such outstanding quality as Hopkins, but we do all have gifts that can be used in the service of God. They may not be as obvious as a gift for writing or art; they may lie in our ability to welcome others, to offer hospitality or kindness to strangers. We may be gifted mathematicians, able to help our church and those in our community for whom finance is a challenge. All we have been given can in turn be given back to the glory of God.

How can we best use the skills and talents that we have been given to forward the purposes of the kingdom?

Gerard Manley Hopkins

God's Grandeur

The world is charged with the grandeur of God.
* It will flame out, like shining from shook foil;*
* It gathers to a greatness, like the ooze of oil*
Crushed. Why do men then now not reck his rod?
Generations have trod, have trod, have trod;
* And all is seared with trade; bleared, smeared with toil;*
* And wears man's smudge and shares man's smell: the soil*
Is bare now, nor can foot feel, being shod.

And, for all this, nature is never spent;
* There lives the dearest freshness deep down things;*
And though the last lights off the black West went
* Oh, morning, at the brown brink eastward, springs—*
Because the Holy Ghost over the bent
World broods with warm breast and with ah! Bright wings.

Wherever Hopkins looked, he saw evidence of the 'grandeur of God', the wonderful variety and beauty of creation, and the vast amount of love that God has poured into that creation. This is an extraordinary and precious gift to possess, and one to which we can all aspire. For this meditation you will need to find something small and beautiful from nature. It can be a stone, a flower, a piece of moss, a twig or some bark—whatever appeals to you. If you can, go outside for your search. Make the search part of the meditation exercise; ask God to bless your search, to give you the vision to seek out the beautiful and the inspirational. When you have found your object, which should fit comfortably into your hand, find a place to rest and stay. This can be outside, where you found the object, or indoors if it is easier for you to focus there.

Hold the object in your hand and look at it closely. Notice how intricate it is, how delicate and varied the colours and patterns. Think of the love that has been poured into its creation, small and unimportant though it appears. Remember that all of God's love is poured into every single part of his creation—this insignificant object is in fact a symbol of the whole world. Remember that just as God has poured his love into this piece of nature, so too he pours out his love upon us; we are cherished and cared for to the utmost extent. Ask God to make you aware of his presence, his Spirit, 'brooding' over the world, like a bird nurses its chicks, keeping his world, and ourselves, safe in his love.

Colours of creation

You will need a paint catalogue (this can be picked up from a DIY store), scissors, a large container, and a carrier bag.

Take your paint catalogue and roughly cut out all the paint samples. Ensure that you have a wide selection of different colours on separate pieces of paper.

Place these colours in a large container, then, without looking, take out six or eight different colours.

Find a place where nature is accessible to you—it could be your local nature reserve or woodland, some fields or a stretch of open country. If you are city-bound, journey to your largest open space or park.

Take some time to settle yourself—look around you and notice carefully what the environment feels like. Listen to the sounds that surround you, both natural and man-made. Become aware of the temperature and air quality, whether hot or cold, damp or dry. Feel yourself at one with the landscape.

Take out your coloured scraps of paper. Ideally you should

have a wide variety of colours. Now try to find objects that match each colour in your hand. Some of these—particularly the green and brown shades—will be easy, others more difficult. Look at any litter or debris for the more garish colours, although you may not wish to pick these up if they appear hazardous. Gather all these coloured objects in your carrier bag and take them home.

At home, spend some time arranging your colours and your objects before you. How successful were you in your quest? Examine the objects you have selected—how many different colours do they contain? Compare them with the flatness of the shades that are on your paint samples. You may wish to read one or two of Hopkins' poems again.

Finding beauty in misshapes

Pied Beauty

> Glory be to God for dappled things—
>   For skies of couple-colour as a brinded cow;
>   For rose-moles all in stipple upon trout that swim;
> Fresh-firecoal chestnut-falls; finches' wings;
>   Landscape plotted and pieced—fold, fallow, and plough;
>   And all trades, their gear and tackle and trim.
>
> All things counter, original, spare, strange;
>   Whatever is fickle, freckled (who knows how?)
>   With swift, slow; sweet, sour; adazzle, dim;
> He fathers-forth whose beauty is past change:
>   Praise him.

Now read Genesis 1:24–25. It is very easy to find God in nature when we are standing in beautiful countryside on a lovely sunny day. It is easy when we are surrounded by spectacular landscape or amazing scenery to thank God for his gift of creation. But how do we react to the ugly, destructive side of nature—to wizened toads, hairy spiders, lank weeds? Do our feelings of revulsion and disgust blind us to the care and skill that went into their creation? The verses in Genesis remind us that God made all creatures, whatever their size, colour or appearance, and that he saw that it was all good, with no exceptions. Hopkins' poem takes up this theme, and reminds us that beauty can be found in the 'strange', the 'slow', the 'sour', the 'dim' as well as in those things that are conventionally attractive. We too can strive to find God's beauty and his love, in all created things, even in those whose appearance is at odds with our own taste and preferences.

Making a word pile

For Hopkins, it was just as important to see beauty in the strange, the ugly, the apparently ill-formed, as it was to find it in those objects traditionally acknowledged to be attractive. We are reminded in 'Pied Beauty' that very often it is the irregularities in objects, the freckles and moles, that give them their individuality and appeal. In this poem, Hopkins piles words upon words in his effort to make us open our eyes to the extraordinary and the unusual objects that surround us, and to appreciate them.

For this exercise, take a natural object, large or small, and spend some time observing it as closely as possible. It could be a tree or a hedge, the sky, a group of hills, or it could be a ladybird, a feather, a blade of grass.

Once you have examined it closely, make a word-pile like Hopkins—that is, try to think of as many different words to describe the object as possible. Don't stick to descriptive words, such as colour or shape: try to set your mind free to think of words and phrases that convey the essence of the object, its attraction for you, what made you choose it, what sets it apart from other, similar objects.

Write these words and phrases on a large piece of paper, using a variety of writing styles. If you have any crayons or coloured pens, you could decorate the page with colours and patterns. When you have run out of ways of describing the object, place it on your word-pile if possible, and thank God.

Hope amongst loss

Binsey Poplars

> My aspens dear, whose airy cages quelled,
> Quelled or quenched in leaves the leaping sun,
> All felled, felled, are all felled;
> Of a fresh and following folded rank
>   Not spared, not one
>   That dandled a sandalled
>   Shadow that swam or sank
> On meadow and river and wind-wandering weed-winding bank.
>
> O if we but knew what we do
> When we delve or hew—
> Hack and rack the growing green!
>   Since country is so tender
> To touch, her being so slender
> That, like this sleek and seeing ball
> But a prick will make no eye at all,
> Where we, even where we mean

> *To mend her we end her,*
> *When we hew or delve:*
> *After-comers cannot guess the beauty been.*
> *Ten or twelve, only ten or twelve*
> *Strokes of havoc unselve*
> *The sweet especial scene,*
> *Rural scene, a rural scene,*
> *Sweet especial rural scene.*

In 1879, having studied at the University of Oxford, Hopkins was sent back to the city after his ordination and acceptance into the Society of Jesus. He made return visits to the places that he loved as a student, and was horrified, on walking out to Binsey, to discover that the avenue of poplar trees leading to the church had been felled. 'Binsey Poplars' is a lyrical expression of loss and regret, not just for the beauty of the trees, but for a longed-for past and a vanished sense of security: 'felled, felled, all are felled'—the words sound like the tolling of a funeral bell, marking a great loss.

It can be both comforting and distressing to find scenes of devastation in nature. When we suffer great pain and anguish, parallel examples of destruction in nature can bring us solace as we see our pain echoed in God's creation, a physical reminder that God shares our pains and sorrows as well as our joys. Similarly, we can find hope for our own eventual recovery in the signs of regeneration and new growth that can always be seen even in the most devastating of natural disasters—seeds of renewal and future perfection in the face of current difficulties and tragedy. Find a 'rural scene', whether real or pictured, and meditate prayerfully on these things.

Gerard Manley Hopkins

Small holy places

The focus of this series of reflections has been to find God in the ordinary, the detail, as well as in the grandeur and the glory. This two-fold approach has a particular use in the spiritual practice of pilgrimage. Pilgrimages usually have as a destination a particular holy place, a church or cathedral or the site of a miracle, but it is the journey that is important, not the destination.

To be able to go on a pilgrimage to one of the major sites is a privilege indeed, but if we are unable to achieve this, we need not abandon the idea of pilgrimage altogether. There is a role for 'small pilgrim places' in our lives. These small pilgrim places can be churches, churchyards, or simply a spot conducive to quiet and meditation. We can journey to them over some hours, or just a few minutes, as long as we spend that time in reflection on the place of Christ in our hearts and our expectation of meeting him in the daily events that make up our lives.

Once arrived, we can give thanks for the stage in our life's journey that we have reached, reflect on our journey so far, and think about the direction we hope our life will take in the future. Then, refreshed by the stillness, we can return to our daily lives, remembering as we do so that we do not make our journey alone but in the company of Christ.

We are very blessed in that this country has hundreds of small pilgrim places in its parish churches. They are places of stillness and peace, made holy by the prayers of thousands of people over hundreds of years. If you can, take the time to visit a small pilgrim place in the heart of your community and rest in the presence of God.

Gerard Manley Hopkins

An appreciation for creation

Read Luke 15:3–7. Hopkins' great gift was his ability to find beauty and wonder in every single aspect of God's creation. He looked at the landscape with the eye of a true artist—he could appreciate the vast expanses of mountain ranges and moorland stretches but he could equally find miracles of creation in the tiniest detail of a bird's feather or the petal of a flower. In this he does no more than reflect that most precious characteristic of God—that of cherishing every single aspect of the world that he made, focusing particularly on each of his children. Those famous parables of lost and found, of a lost sheep, a lost pearl, a lost coin, serve to focus our attention on this aspect of God's great love—so great that it can sustain a universe, so detailed that it not only notices when one of his children is lost, but can devote all the time and attention that is necessary to draw it back into the fold.

What can we do in return? We can appreciate God's creation indeed. But we can do more than that. We can find the evidence of his love and his divine attention not only in our surroundings but also in those who people those surroundings. For Hopkins did not reserve his gift of observation and appreciation just for the things of nature—he too reminds us that we must see the face of Christ in those we meet in our daily lives, for it is in recognising the value of every individual that we will truly recognise God.

> *For Christ plays in ten thousand places,*
> *Lovely in limbs, and lovely in eyes not his*
> *To the Father through the features of men's faces.*
> AS KINGFISHERS CATCH FIRE

Gerard Manley Hopkins

Collage of faces

You will need: as many newspapers and magazines as you can find (the more illustrated the better), scissors, a glue stick, a large piece of paper, pencil or pen.

There is a very famous portrait of Christ that from a distance simply shows the face of Jesus. However, on closer examination, it is observed that this face is in fact made up of hundreds of smaller portraits, reminding us that the face of Christ can be seen in all those whom we meet in our daily lives.

Using your pen or pencil, draw a large outline of a face on the paper. It can be as simple or as complicated as you like—don't worry about whether it looks lifelike or not; this exercise is a prayer, not an art class! Go through your magazines and papers and cut out all the images of faces you find. Glue these faces on to the large face you have drawn, using the darker and lighter images to depict eyes and mouth, hair and other features.

When you have completed your collage, look at it and try to hold in your vision both the large face and the smaller ones contained within it. Ask God for the grace to see Christ playing in 'ten thousand places', to see 'the Father through the features of men's faces'.

Why do sinners' ways prosper?

Thou art indeed just, Lord, if I contend
With thee; but, sir, so what I plead is just.
Why do sinners ways' prosper? and why must
Disappointment all I endeavour end?

Wert thou my enemy, O thou my friend,
How wouldst thou worse, I wonder than thou dost

Defeat, thwart me? Oh the sots and thralls of lust
Do in spare hours more thrive than I that spend,
Sir, life upon thy cause? See, banks and brakes
Now, leavèd how thick! lacèd they are again
With fretty chervil, look, and fresh wind shakes
Them; birds build—but not I build; no, but strain,
Time's eunuch, and not breed one work that wakes.
Mine, O thou lord of life, send my roots rain.

You will need: a jug of water, and a dish of dry soil. If you cannot access these, find a picture of a desert or wilderness and another of a field ready for harvest, or a similar picture of abundance of produce. Place these side by side in front of you.

'Why do sinners prosper?' is a cry that is as human as it is universal, one that has been echoed throughout the ages, lamented over in the Psalms, railed against in Job, and is still asked by us today. Why do the things we do so often end in disaster, when those efforts of other, less worthy people, seem to be ringed with triumph? Hopkins echoes our thoughts of despair and anger when he demands from God an answer to his questions. Why do idle, lazy people, who devote their time to worldly activities and pursuits, seem to achieve more than he does, when he spends all his time trying to serve God? In a time of creative drought, Hopkins looks with despair on those who are achieving so much more than he is, and cries out to God for the refreshing rain of inspiration and purpose that only God can provide.

How often have we gazed with envy on the achievements of others, and felt resentment that we are denied success? How many times have we felt we were walking in a desert, whether emotional or spiritual? How many times have we thirsted for the recognition or acceptance, the love or renown that we feel we deserve? Place your hands in the dish of dry soil, feel how harsh it is under your fingers. Nothing seems to be growing; there appears to be no life. Slowly pour some of the water from the jug into the soil and mix it in with your fingers. Do not be afraid to get your hands dirty—you cannot create conditions that enable the nourishing and sustaining of life without effort or toil. Look now at the soil—it is ready for sowing. It may already contain the seeds of plants that needed only water to begin to germinate and grow. Think of the desert times in your life—how often did they contain the seeds for future growth? Think too of the times when the achievements and knowledge of others have helped you on your way—they needed to grow first before you could achieve your own potential. Thank God for times of drought and for times of plenty, and ask him for the grace to celebrate the gifts of others as well as your own.

Society of Jesus

Gerard Manley Hopkins was a member of the Society of Jesus, founded by Ignatius of Loyola (1491–1556). The youngest of eleven children, Ignatius left his home in the Basque region of Spain to become a page for a nobleman. His life of brawling, gambling and womanising was disrupted when his master lost his position. Ignatius then joined the army but was subsequently badly wounded in the leg and taken prisoner in France. During his year's incarceration, while he was recovering from his injury, he turned away from his previous life and towards God. Then, inspired by a vision of the Virgin Mary and Christ, he spent some years in retreat, writing his famous work, *The Spiritual Exercises*. In 1534, Ignatius and six other men formed the Society of Jesus, using the Spiritual Exercises as the foundation for their spirituality, and vowing poverty, chastity and obedience. Ignatius spent much time as an administrator over the Jesuits, and had the new order emphasise preaching, education and acts of charity. Today, the Society of Jesus describes its mission as the service of faith and the promotion in society of 'that justice of the Gospel which is the embodiment of God's love and saving mercy'. Outside the order, followers of Ignatian spirituality use meditation and retreats to encounter God and discover in the Bible his message for their lives and mission.

A prayer of St Ignatius

Teach us, good Lord, to serve you as you deserve; to give and not to count the cost; to fight and not to heed the wounds; to toil and not to seek for rest; to labour and not to ask for any reward, save that of knowing that we do your will.
Amen

13–26 OCTOBER

The wisdom of God

Janet Fletcher

Wisdom and Sophia?

We all have our own inner wisdom—a wisdom that is handed down to us through our families, through the culture and heritage of the places where we live, through the conversations we share in and all that is experienced by us year by year; an inner wisdom too, that evolves through our faith, and the ever deepening of a relationship with God.

The Greek word for wisdom is 'Sophia', and so grammatically wisdom takes on the feminine rather than the masculine. We discover in Proverbs and in the Apocrypha that wisdom is either 'her' or 'she'. It may be that this enables the possibility of a different approach or way of discerning, and praying to, God. Yet, the wisdom of God is far more than a gender-related word; it speaks of embodiment, presence, touch, of Christ with us, and the Spirit flowing within our daily lives. In wisdom there is gentleness and strength, vulnerability and courage. This means that wisdom can refer to the quality of life lived out and our way of understanding and relating to life. It also signifies the Divine, of God.

Wisdom has so many facets to her. Wisdom is not only about knowledge and understanding, but is also about an openness and willingness to seek out the God within. The Wisdom of God involves a journey of self-discovery and self-knowing; a search for our own 'I am'. There is much to explore around the theme of wisdom and Sophia. As a beginning to this exploration, think about these questions:

Does the thought of wisdom/Sophia in the feminine cause any problem to you? If the answer is yes, then please feel free to think and pray in the way that is best for you.

What words, images or thoughts does 'wisdom' bring to mind?

Wisdom in the Proverbs

Read Proverbs 3:13–18. What are the thoughts that initially come to you from reading this passage? It begins and ends with the word 'blessed', or, in some translations, 'happy'. Happiness can be described in many ways and can also depend upon how we are feeling, and how we understand what it is to be happy. The word 'blessed' is perhaps more related to the sense of 'counting our blessings' or that spiritual understanding of being blessed in our faith, and by God's presence in our lives. How much of a similarity is there between them, or how large a gap is there from your own understanding and interpretation of those two words?

Paradoxically, we can be both happy, or blessed, and sad at the same time. Life is going well, but occasionally we see, hear or experience something that brings reality home to us. Wisdom draws together both the ups and downs of life.

The passage also says that to follow wisdom is to follow the path of peace, a way that is described as being a very pleasant pathway. Many times our path through life is 'pleasant', while at other times it doesn't feel that way.

How would you describe your life at this moment? Is it one of peace, happiness and pleasantness? Do you feel blessed in your life?

The passage says that wisdom is more precious than jewels and that 'nothing you desire can compare with her'. What is precious to you? What do you desire at this moment?

The tree of life

In Proverbs 3:13–18, we read that wisdom is 'a tree of life to those who lay hold of her' (v. 18). A tree has many roots, which tunnel their way deep into the ground and the soil in which they have been planted. There they find the initial nourishment they need for growth. As the tree grows into maturity, it will need both the sun and the rain to continue to nurture its growth, if it is to fulfil its purpose and potential. We too need to be nourished and nurtured if we are to fulfil our purpose and potential in life.

In a time of quietness and prayer, gather before you a large piece of paper, pencils and crayons.

On the paper, draw the outline of a tree. The tree can be as basic or elaborate as you wish it to be. Draw roots going into the soil, and branches coming out from the main trunk.

Once you have the outline, take time to become quiet and still with God. In prayerfulness ask that the wisdom of God will be with you, to guide you and illuminate the prayer you seek as you look at the tree of your life.

Spend time pondering over the influences and words of wisdom that have guided you in faith, and write these at the roots.

What sustains your life of faith? What words of wisdom help you now? Write these at the trunk of the tree.

Ponder over all that needs to be nurtured, or has been nurtured in your life of faith, and write these into leaves drawn on to one side of the tree.

On the other side of the tree, draw leaves and write in them the possibilities and potential in your life in general, which may include life in church as well.

Afterwards, spend some time reflecting on all that has been prayed and written. Is there anything that you may need to pray about again, or speak to someone about?

Wisdom and prayer

There are many ways of praying with passages from the Bible. One way is the *lectio divina*. This is a slow reading of a passage until a word or a phrase seems important. Then, it is to stay with that word or phrase, repeating it slowly and silently, allowing it to journey deep within, until it feels right either to move on to the rest of the passage again, or to draw the time of prayer to a close. This is a way of prayer that can bring us close to the wisdom of God and the wisdom of our own inner life and faith.

To begin this time of prayer, find a space where you are undisturbed and comfortable. Find Proverbs 3:13–18. Take time to become still and quiet, to put aside the thoughts of the present moment and any cares and concerns you have by asking God to hold them for you. Slowly, breathing gently, begin to relax the body, to breathe out any tension and to breathe in God's peace and wisdom. Slowly, pray through the whole of the body from the top of the head to the tips of the toes, taking as much time as you wish. There is no need to rush.

Slowly, read through Proverbs 3:13–18 and stay with the word or phrase that seems important to you. Prayerfully and quietly seek God within the words and phrases of the passage.

Afterwards, reflect upon the time of prayer, the words or phrases that came to you, your understanding of them, anything you may have felt, and make a note of any thoughts you may wish to return to at another time.

The wisdom of God

Seeking God's wisdom

In all that I seek to do in my life:
God of all that is, God of all Creation,

May wisdom's presence bring enlightenment and peace.

In my prayers for my family and my friends:
God of all that is, God of all Creation,

May wisdom's presence bring enlightenment and peace.

In my seeking to understand my call from you:
God of all that is, God of all Creation,

May wisdom's presence bring enlightenment and peace.

In my hopes for the future:
God of all that is, God of all Creation,

May wisdom's presence bring enlightenment and peace.

In my ups and downs of life:
God of all that is, God of all Creation,

May wisdom's presence bring enlightenment and peace.

In my prayers for this world:
God of all that is, God of all Creation,

May wisdom's presence bring enlightenment and peace.

In my journey of faith:
God of all that is, God of all Creation,

May wisdom's presence bring enlightenment and peace.

In my prayers for all that needs to be nurtured and nourished in my life:
God of all that is, God of all Creation,

May wisdom's presence bring enlightenment and peace.

Wisdom and friendship

The Apocrypha also contains writings on the words of wisdom. In the book of Sirach we read, 'Wisdom teaches her children and gives help to those who seek her' (4:11, NRSV). In a later chapter she speaks of friendship, saying, 'Faithful friends are a sturdy shelter: whoever finds one has found a treasure. Faithful friends are beyond price; no amount can balance their worth. Faithful friends are life-saving medicine; and those who fear the Lord will find them. Those who fear the Lord direct their friendship aright, for as they are, so are their neighbours also' (6:14–17).

The saying 'You can't choose your family but you can choose

your friends' is probably familiar, although of course within many families there can also be found friendship. What is friendship, and what does it mean to have friends and be a friend?

Wisdom says she will help all who seek her. This gives to us one element of friendship, that of support and help; to be a helpmate. True friends are to be treasured, for their worth in our lives is beyond a price tag. A friend is there for us, to be a shelter of care, love and peace in times of difficulty, and to share in our joy and life-changing moments. In Jesus, and in his teaching, we have the image and imprint of the true friend—a friend who believes in us, wants the best for us, and will not forsake us.

In a time of prayer, become quiet and still within. In your prayer ask Jesus to be present with you. Look upon Jesus as a friend at your side, and quietly and slowly offer to him in prayer the names of your friends, and the qualities that drew you to them in friendship. End the time of prayer by giving thanks to God. Then return to your 'tree of life' and add some or all of the names of the friends you prayed about, and one special quality they each have.

Wisdom and Emmanuel

John's Gospel opens with words that reflect the indwelling presence of the Word within us. 'In the beginning was the Word, and the Word was with God, and the Word was God... The Word became flesh and made his dwelling among us' (1:1, 14). Later on in his Gospel, John brings to us the Word that becomes Spirit so that we may know for ourselves the presence of the trinitarian God with us.

As we draw ever closer to Advent, the image of the incarnation, of Emmanuel, who is God with us, begins to speak slowly into our lives and our prayers through the liturgy and readings. Here we see the wonder and the amazing truth of God's wisdom revealed in love to us, as the Son born into the human world who takes on our humanity. In the resurrection, the Spirit is poured upon us, to dwell within us, filling us with the love of God to lead us deeper into faith.

One way to consider the touch and presence of the Spirit, and of his wisdom, is through this embodiment of Christ in us. In a time when you know you won't be disturbed, and with paper and crayons, settle into the quietness of prayer. Begin by becoming outwardly still, letting go of any tension or concerns. Then slowly and prayerfully seek to journey into the core of your being, searching out the indwelling presence of God. Prayerfully reflect upon the images and words that come to you. When you feel ready, write and draw those words and images on to the paper. These may appear to be random words or simply swirls of colours but they are a part of your prayer and the God who dwells within.

What is our inner wisdom?

Wisdom is not only about knowledge and understanding but embraces the tough and the painful, the stresses and the joys of daily living, and it holds as one our giftedness and our limitations. To come to know our inner wisdom is to come to know the whole person as we are known by God, 'warts and all'! This inner wisdom is not a wisdom we are born with, but evolves throughout our lives. We discover the presence of God's wisdom through the mistakes we make and learn from and through listening to others.

There is so much that has enabled our own inner wisdom to grow and inform the way we live. For example, our history and heritage, culture and the society in which we live, the faith and tradition of church to which we belong and our journey with God, through our family, friends and relationships, our educational years, working life and leisure time, the experiences we have that touch and shape us, those that are personal and those that derive from world events, the books we read, the music to which we listen.

Look again at your 'tree of life' in a time of quiet prayer. Quietly reflect on the influences upon your life, and think about those who have shared with you their inner wisdom. With thanksgiving, offer these in prayer to God, and write them on to your 'tree of life', maybe adding them on to the ground around the tree, representing something of the ground of who you are as a person today.

Weaving in our inner wisdom

Our inner wisdom and God's wisdom can reach into the creative areas of our lives; likewise our prayer too can be offered creatively and without any need for artistic perfection! Weaving, with pieces of wool or ribbon, or even strips of coloured paper of different textures, can be both prayerful and calming.

Before beginning this time of prayer, gather around you different coloured bits of wool, ribbon, paper, and a pair of scissors. The idea is to use a small branch fallen from a tree (about twelve to 18 inches) that has a couple of offshoots coming out from the main branch. Alternatively, a wooden or metal mug tree will be just as effective.

Decide upon a theme for your prayer. This may be remembering the people who have helped to shape your life, your own giftedness, or how you feel life is for you at the present moment.

Take a little time to become quiet and still, to seek out your own inner wisdom and the touch of wisdom/Sophia. When you are ready, take a piece of wool or ribbon, tie one end around a part of the branch and thread it through the 'branches' or wrap it around the branch, securing the end. Then, with as many pieces as you like, weave them through until you feel you are finished. As you weave, think about the colours and textures used for each part of the prayer, and who or what they represent to you. There is no right or wrong way of weaving this prayer. All that is created by you is as unique as your prayer, your own inner wisdom, and the creativity of wisdom in your life.

Spend some time reflecting upon the prayer, your thoughts and feelings, and offer those too to God.

Wisdom's story and song

The poem below brings to us the song of wisdom in our lives and being, a guide through the ups and downs of life, and all that is experienced. Read through the poem, and then quietly re-read it, reflecting upon all that is happening in your life at this time, where wisdom may be needed, the joys and the storms being experienced, and where and how wisdom may be calling out to you.

> *From the heights, to the very depths,*
> *from the treetops and mountain peaks*
> *to the deepest root and underground cavern*
> *Sophia sings her story, seeking, searching, and sustaining*
> *each and every fibre of being and life,*
> *speaking her story, her wisdom,*
> *to touch, to weave, to reveal the eternal story*
> *of faith imprinted within, where words heard*

> *mingle with experiences felt, understanding learnt,*
> *questions asked, hopes and dreams lie alongside fears and*
> *anxieties.*
> *Wisdom Sophia embracing all, against each windswept*
> *stormy day and night,*
> *each passing moment of remembered joy and love and*
> *laughter,*
> *each dry and arid passage of time,*
> *each fulfilled and fruitful moment.*
> *Wisdom's song echoes and sings within — revealing,*
> *unwrapping*
> *the layers of her ancient story,*
> *from the heights to the depths*
> *of all that was,*
> *and is now,*
> *and is yet to be.*

The wisdom of Solomon

Within the Apocrypha we discover the writing attributed to Solomon in which he explores and shares his love and respect for the presence and power of wisdom. When called to be king after his father David, Solomon asked God for the wisdom to fulfil his role. He sought the wisdom of understanding and justice when dealing with the problems the people brought to him, and the knowledge of discerning right from wrong.

He writes: 'Therefore I prayed, and understanding was given me; I called on God, and the spirit of wisdom came to me' (Wisdom 7:7, NRSV). 'For wisdom is more mobile than any motion; because of her pureness she pervades and penetrates all things. For she is a breath of the power of God, and a pure emanation of the glory of the Almighty... in every generation she passes into holy souls and makes them friends of God, and prophets; for God loves nothing so much as the person who lives with wisdom' (7:24–25, 27–28).

If you have a Bible with the Apocrypha, read through chapter 7 to discover more of Solomon's thoughts on wisdom.

The images of wisdom from Solomon stretch our imaginations towards a colour-filled and all-pervasive creative presence of God within us and within creation. She comes to breathe into our lives, seeking to reveal our potential, searching our hearts and encouraging a deeper relationship with God.

For Solomon the way of seeking wisdom was through prayer, and through prayer came the touch of God's wisdom into his life. In a time of quietness, write your own prayer of thanksgiving and praise to God, using words which express your own understanding of wisdom. At the same time you may find it helpful to add a few more threads of ribbon or wool to your weaving prayer around a branch.

Wisdom's journey

Paul, writing to the Corinthians, proclaims that all wisdom comes from God, and our own seeking to be wise is at times foolishness. Wisdom comes through living the spiritual life and seeking the mind of Christ (see 1 Corinthians 1:18—2:16).

Here, the varied aspects of wisdom are woven together. Our understanding and knowledge, and how that is used by us, is related to the faith we live by. Faith and our relationship with God will in turn inform the way in which we use our knowledge and understanding; the way we live in the world. For both, and to keep both connected to each other, there needs to be prayer.

What are your thoughts now on wisdom—our gaining of

understanding and knowledge, and of wisdom—the touch and presence of God?

Through these passages, have any particular aspects of wisdom revealed something new to you?

May wisdom inspire my heart to prayer.
May wisdom guide my thoughts into honest speech.
May wisdom draw my knowledge into deeper understanding.
May wisdom sweep through my inner being to bring forgiveness.
May wisdom kindle the flame of love within into a fire of deepening faith.
May wisdom guide my journey to God, and beyond.
Amen

27 OCTOBER–9 NOVEMBER

The message of Jeremiah

Sally Smith

Introduction

Jeremiah was a prophet, called by God to bring God's word to a nation that had well and truly turned its back on God. The message Jeremiah brings is not an easy one. He tells the nation how it will be taken over, how Jerusalem will be defeated and the people will be exiled. He reminds them of what God has done for them in the past and that he still loves them. In chapter 5, God says if there was just one person left who acted justly and sought the truth, he would listen and save the whole city. Jeremiah had a difficult job: not one person was willing to listen, and so in chapter 20 Jeremiah reaches the point where he declares, 'Cursed be the day I was born! May the day my mother bore me not be blessed!' (20:14).

But in the midst of this message of God's anger, we see other aspects of God; we see his love for Jeremiah and for the people and his desire for good for them. After the message of destruction comes the prophecy of how God will restore the people to their land and how his anger will be stilled. So, we can read of the God who loves us, who wants us to turn to him, who calls us. We are reminded of his faithfulness and love for us, which is as true now as in the time Jeremiah was bringing God's message.

To get a taste of the whole book of Jeremiah, you might like to read the following passages: 7:1–29; 29:4–14; 31:31–34; 39:1–10.

Before I formed you

> *'Before I formed you in the womb I knew you,*
> *and before you were born I consecrated you;*
> *I appointed you a prophet to the nations.'*
>
> JEREMIAH 1:5, NRSV

Jeremiah was appointed prophet, not after an interview or because he turned out to have certain skills that would be useful for a prophet. Jeremiah was a prophet because that was what God had always intended. Before he was born, God knew Jeremiah would be a prophet and that he would be suited to being a prophet.

God knew Jeremiah, as he also knew you and me, before we were born, even before we were being formed in the womb. Pause and consider this: before you were in the womb, before one cell of you existed, God knew you and loved you, and consecrated you for his work! Allow that to sink in and begin to accept what this says about God and about you.

We are not all called to be prophets. For some it is not as clear what they are called to do as it was for Jeremiah. One thing is clear: we are all called to be the person God intends us to be; his servant, doing his work, whatever that might be. You are not called to be Jeremiah, but you are called to be you.

Spend some time with Jeremiah 1:5. It might help to imagine going back through your life with God. Together, remember some of the key events and moments you have shared, or times and places you have not allowed God in before. He was there in all of them. Imagine going back before the earliest time you can remember. Allow God to take you back and show you the time before you were born and before you existed. Allow him to show how much he has longed for your life and wanted to share everything with you, the good and the not so good. Feel his excitement for each moment of your life.

Recognise how it feels to know that God has known you longer than anyone else has.

God continues to call us; it is a life-long process. How are you allowing this to happen at this stage of your life?

If you do not have a clear sense of calling in your life, recognise how you are responding to his call to be you and how you allow this to come about.

I am only...

Jeremiah 1:6–10

In response to the call from God, Jeremiah said, 'I do not know how to speak for I am only a boy' (Jeremiah 1:6).

We do not always see the potential that God sees in us. In the Bible, in people we know and in ourselves, we see examples of God calling and people saying, 'But I'm not worthy, I'm only...'

When the angel told Mary that she was to have a son who would be called the Son of the most high, she had a question, though hers was the more practical question of how this could happen.

Are there areas where you are resisting God's call at the moment? Or areas you are not sure about? What is your 'but I am only...'? Or do you, like Mary, have a more practical question? Tell these to God. Allow him to touch these areas as he touched Jeremiah's mouth.

Are you able to say with Mary, 'Here am I, the servant of the Lord; let it be with me according to your word' (Luke 1:38)?

Tree planted by the river
Jeremiah 17:7–8

This image of a tree beside the stream comes in comparison to the image of a bush in the desert in the preceding verses. The shrub clings to life, often looking more dead than alive. There is nothing to feed it, to give it nourishment. The tree by the stream, like the bush in the desert, is in full sun, but it has its roots in the stream, a continuously revitalising source of refreshment and nourishment. The tree is therefore able to produce much fruit to feed others.

Imagine a tree planted beside a stream. You might like to draw a tree, with roots that reach deep down, drawing up water. Feel that movement of drawing up and refreshment of the fresh water. What is the water that feeds you? How do you reach into it as the tree roots reach out to the stream?

Add some branches and leaves to your tree. Leaves give shade but are dependent on the water for growth. In times of drought trees may lose their leaves to preserve their resources.

What is the fruit of your life? You might like to draw some fruit on your tree and write what they represent. Is it an abundant harvest?

To trust in God means that when the heat is on, there is no need to fear. What might you fear at the moment? How is the stream overcoming these fears? Draw the sun and name those fears, then allow the leaves to shade you from that fear.

Spend time 'drinking' from the stream and acknowledging your trust in God.

You shall be called

Jeremiah 20:3

The response of Pashhur, a priest, to Jeremiah's prophecy was to have him beaten and put in the stocks overnight. Pashhur's reward for this act was to have God change his name to 'Terror-all-around'. In the previous chapter (19:1–9) we read how and why Topheth becomes known as the valley of Slaughter.

Others can see us very differently from how we see ourselves, and if allowed to name us may come up with some surprising suggestions. They may suggest In Control, when we feel we are inwardly panicking, or Compassion, when we know the effort it has taken to show compassion we are not feeling, or Angry, without allowing for the catalogue of disasters that have beset us…

God would give us yet another name, seeing us in a different way. In Jeremiah 23:6 the king is to be called 'The Lord our righteousness'. In Isaiah 62:4 God changes the name of his people from Forsaken to My Delight Is in Her, and their land from Desolate to Married.

What names do you carry for yourself? Don't judge the use of these names; accept them as part of you and who you are.

When you are ready, turn to God. Tell him the names you wear. Then ask him what names he uses for you, or try My Delight Is in You as a name for you from God.

Receive the new name. How does it feel? Like a new item of clothing, try it for size and fit; does it suit you? Get used to it and how it feels to be known by this name and all that the name brings with it. Return to this new name over the coming days.

If you know the song 'I will change your name', you could play it or sing it to finish your prayer time. Are there other new names God is trying to give you?

House of the potter

There are several symbolic actions recorded in Jeremiah that give extra weight to the words he speaks. God may tell him to go to a specific place, or take an object and perform an action with it. (See 13:1–11, 12–14; 24; 27:1–11 for examples.)

Perhaps the best known of these symbolic actions is God's instruction to Jeremiah in chapter 18:2, 'Go down to the potter's house…'

Imagine the scene. Jeremiah arrives at the potter's house. See the stacks of everyday earthenware pots outside. They are waiting to be used. Sitting inside the doorway is the potter beside his simple treadle-powered wheel. Watch as he works the clay into the shape of a pot, and then all goes wrong and he gathers the clay back into a ball. Watch as he works it back together, reforming the solid ball of clay and rethrowing it. Watch as he shapes the clay and a new pot emerges from that lump of clay. The potter handles the clay carefully and skilfully until the pot is completed. See the look of satisfaction with his work as he places it to dry.

God says to you, 'I can do that with you. You are in my hands, and like the potter I can reshape you, I can build you up and mould and form you.'

Are you able to allow God to mould you as the potter moulds the clay?

What do you say to God in response?

You might like to spend some time with some clay, or play dough, or even bread dough or Blu-tak™. Play with it, mould it and then reform it. As you manipulate it, allow God to be moulding and forming you gently with his strong hands.

The yoke

Another of the symbolic actions in Jeremiah is the yoke. God calls Jeremiah to make a wooden yoke and to wear it to show how the people can be yoked to the king of Babylon. The alternative, he explains, is destruction. Hananiah, a false prophet, breaks Jeremiah's yoke, calling him a false prophet and for this Hananiah is yoked with an iron yoke and dies within a year (see Jeremiah 28).

Jeremiah was clearly yoked with God, living his life obeying and trusting him. It was not an easy yoke; he was called to say some difficult things and his life was sometimes in danger. It was a lonely place to be, but it was in the yoke that he was joined to God and was working for and with him.

Two people or animals together in a yoke need to work very closely together to make the yoke an effective tool. They need to be heading in the same direction and at the same pace, or they will veer off course and it will be hard work.

We can choose with whom we are to be yoked.

Imagine the day ahead of you. (Look in your diary if this helps.) Imagine going through the day yoked with God. As you go out and meet people, work, shop, and so on, God is there next to you; you can't escape him. How might you behave differently, knowing that God is so close? What will you change today, knowing you are yoked with God? What will you share with God that will make the day easier?

Jesus said, 'For my yoke is easy and my burden is light' (Matthew 11:30). We can submit to that yoke, or we can fight it.

You might like to tie a thread around your wrist as a reminder today that you are tied to God in a yoke, and that you are both pulling in the same direction.

Plans

> *'For surely I know the plans I have for you, says the Lord, plans for your welfare and not for harm, to give you a future with hope.'*
> JEREMIAH 29:11

The people don't listen to Jeremiah and end up in exile in Babylon. Jeremiah doesn't give up on them, and he writes a letter to them in exile. In the letter he tells them that after 70 years, God will visit them and bring them back to Jerusalem. In the meantime, they are to get on with building and planting, marrying and having children, so that they will increase in number and prosper.

They will have to wait 70 years, but after that time, as Julian of Norwich was to say many years later, 'All shall be well, and all shall be well, and all manner of things shall be well.'

God's love for his people had not waned. He was still planning and preparing a future for them, even when they had turned from him and rejected him. God plans a future for us, with a hope and our welfare in mind, even if it sometimes doesn't feel like that.

Write down the names of the next few days (Monday, Tuesday, Wednesday…).

What do you know of God's plans for you over these days? What do you want, need or expect from God?

Now write the names of the next few months (November, December, January…).

What do you anticipate being in God's plans for these months?

What about the next few years?

How might God continue providing for you? What would you ask from him?

Everlasting love

> '*I have loved you with an everlasting love; therefore I have continued my faithfulness to you.*'
>
> JEREMIAH 31:3

The beginning of this verse is on a silver band I regularly wear on a chain round my neck. The first part of the verse was important to me during a retreat several years ago, and I still have the words above my desk. In the months following the retreat, it was the second part of the verse that kept me going; God continued his faithfulness to me during what became a very difficult year. Unlike the people of Israel, I knew God's love and faithfulness through this period and was able to hold on (often physically with my necklace) to that love and faithfulness.

I invite you to create a symbol of this everlasting love.

Take a strip of paper about 2 cm wide and the length of a piece of A4. On one side write, 'I have loved you with an everlasting love.' On the other side, starting from the same end, write, 'therefore I have continued my faithfulness to you.'

Join the ends to make a ring, but before you stick them together, turn one of the ends over; the writing from one side should now follow on from the writing on the other side, making a continuous band. Follow the words with your finger as you read them, going round and repeating them. Follow the words round and round, receiving them again and again. Recognise that God will continue saying them to you, forever. Begin to enter that everlasting love.

Hope for the future

God looks forward to the time when his people will return from exile. They will celebrate and praise God and enjoy returning to their own country and building new lives there.

Read Jeremiah 31:1–26 slowly. If a word or phrase catches you, stay with it, receiving it as a gift from God. Try not to analyse it, but allow it to settle deep inside you. Make it yours.

Then, when you are ready, move on until the next word or phrase catches you, and stay a while with it. You might not get very far through the passage in one session, and that's fine; just take the gifts God gives you in the time you have.

I will be your God

Jeremiah 30:22

After the people have gone to Babylon, God tells them about how he will restore their fortunes and they shall return. He promises them: 'And you shall be my people, and I will be your God.'

We, too, are called to be the people of God. But what does that mean?

On a piece of paper write words and phrases that describe what it means to you to belong to the people of God, to be called the people of God, by God. What does God expect of his people?

Spend some time sifting these words. If a particular word creates a response in you, stay with that word. What of God or yourself are you encountering in that word?

God also says, 'and I will be your God'. On another sheet of paper, do a similar exercise exploring what it means for God to be your God. What do you expect of God? Again, spend some time with these words and phrases, responding to the God who is your God and who calls you to be his.

Blessings

Jeremiah was given a hard task that lasted a long time. He was asked to bring a difficult message to the people of God and to remain loyal to them and to keep giving them the message, even when he wasn't being heard. But in his loyalty to God's call, Jeremiah drew closer to God. Many of the passages we have been looking at are ones in which God is telling Jeremiah where he has been and will be in the future in Jeremiah's life, and that is in the centre of it all. God does not leave Jeremiah to cope with this on his own; he is there with him, and has been from the beginning of eternity. Jeremiah is reminded of the good things God has given him and of his love and plans for Jeremiah. These are passages of hope even in the midst of God's despair over his people, and at the centre of it all is the relationship between God and Jeremiah.

Jeremiah was able to bless God's people because he himself was blessed by God. He gave to the people from the riches God had given him. As we leave Jeremiah, it would be good to pause and think of the ways in which you have been blessed as you have walked with Jeremiah. What stands out for you from this time? If you keep a journal, you might look back and see what has been happening. Be reminded of the things God has given you and look at them with God, as you might look at photos with a friend or family member. Remember together the good times and the hard times. Allow God to remind you of the things that have been important to him.

Then, having received blessings from God, reflect on how you will bless others today. What could you say to someone else or do for them that would give them a glimpse of the God who stayed by Jeremiah?

Henri Nouwen says, 'The voice that calls us the Beloved will give us words to bless others and reveal to them that they are no less blessed than we are' (*The Life of the Beloved*, Henri Nouwen, Hodder and Stoughton, 2002, p. 67).

How will you reveal their blessedness to the people you meet today?

10–23 NOVEMBER

The faithfulness of God

Jean Sims

The greatness of God's faithfulness

In this section we shall be exploring something of the nature of God's faithfulness and some of the images that have been used to help us understand more deeply this wonderful characteristic.

Some favourite verses in the Bible about God's faithfulness are from the book of Lamentations. Many hymn and songwriters have responded to them with tunes and words that are used and loved by many people.

> *The steadfast love of the Lord never ceases,*
> *his mercies never come to an end;*
> *they are new every morning;*
> *great is your faithfulness.*
>
> LAMENTATIONS 3:22–23, NRSV

You might already find that you are singing, either silently or out loud, a setting that you know of this or the words in another translation or a paraphrase of these verses. As you do so, you are already thanking and praising God, however you might be feeling.

Now ask God to help you look back over your life. Where have you seen God's faithfulness and continuing loving compassion and constancy?

Prayerfully choose some beads or buttons, each a different colour or shape, reminding you of a particular time of God's faithfulness, maybe through people or events, or maybe something you have heard or seen or felt. If it takes time for you to remember, ask God, 'Please show me.'

Thread the buttons or beads on a length of string or cord. After securing the end, move them along the cord, 'telling' the beads as you name God's faithfulness in your life.

Alternatively, you might chose to place shells, fir cones or other small objects in front of you, moving them as you name what they are symbolising.

'Do you remember when…?' can be a helpful prayer as you do this. Of course God remembers, but this prayer can bring a powerful sense of being together with God in the past and in the present moment and bringing them together in the here and now with you and God. The beads or pebbles could be left in a special prayer space, if you have one, or somewhere where you can notice what you have made or arranged, as you go about your day doing other things, remembering with God in your daily life.

Waiting for God

Waiting is very much part of everyday life; so much so that railway and bus stations, doctors' surgeries and hospital outpatients' departments usually have waiting areas or rooms. Often we find waiting difficult, knowing increasing impatience in a traffic jam or when a bus is late, or growing anxiety or fear as we wait for medical or examination results. There is also the hopeful impatience that can be felt when waiting for good news, such as the birth of a baby.

The writer of Lamentations talks of a deeper waiting, a waiting for God who is faithful in his goodness, a God who can be yearned for and sought after, as someone who is 'my portion', one in whom we have hope (see 3:24–26).

Read these verses, then sit in a comfortable relaxed position, maybe with hands cupped, open and waiting on your lap, or holding an empty bowl. Ask God, who knows precisely what you need, to fill your empty hands or bowl with a portion of himself.

Ask: 'What is it you are wanting to give me today? Here I am, ready and willing, waiting for you.'

Spend a few moments enjoying sitting with God, quietly waiting and listening with your inner self. Then give thanks that God, in his faithfulness, has honoured this time, whether you have felt anything or not.

Of course this can be done in the privilege of a designated prayer time, but also a few moments can be spent in this way at other times and places, such as while waiting for a hospitalised friend to be medically examined, or sitting on a railway station platform.

Anna and Simeon recognise God's faithfulness

In Luke 2:25–38 we read about two people, Simeon and Anna, who have waited to see 'the Lord's Messiah' as God had promised. There is a strong sense that both of them are close to and open to God. Simeon is described as 'righteous and devout'. The Holy Spirit has revealed to him that he will see the promised Messiah before he dies, and he obeys the prompting of the Holy Spirit to go to the temple. Anna, we are told, is an 84-year-old widow, a prophetess, who spends all her time worshipping in the temple, fasting and praying.

When Mary and Joseph bring the small child Jesus to the temple 'to present him to the Lord' (v. 22), both Simeon and Anna recognise who he really is and what his future role will be.

God has kept his promise and they are both full of thanksgiving and praise.

Imaginative contemplation is a way of entering into this story more deeply with the heart as well as the head, allowing the God who is with you today to speak to you in a fresh way.

Carefully read Luke 2:25–38. Then, putting it aside, ask Jesus to be with you as you begin to imagine the scene. Do not be concerned about seeing it as it was in the first century AD. It is being open to God at this moment that is important. You may find that you are watching the scene as yourself or that you become one of the characters, or you may shift from 'becoming' one person to another as the story unfolds. Maybe you will even see it from God's point of view. Just go with the flow. It is all in God's keeping.

These prompts might help: in your imagination picture the scene, noticing what you can see, hear and smell; the weather and the people crowding into the temple. Simeon is there, alert as to why the Holy Spirit has led him to this spot at this particular time. How is he feeling? What is he thinking? Is he searching or waiting? See Mary and Joseph, carrying Jesus, come nearer. They meet. How do they react to Simeon's words? Now Anna joins them. She gives thanks and prophesies. What do they feel and think? Spend time with the baby, who is the centre of all this. As the family, Simeon and Anna leave, and when you are ready, thank God and return to the present.

Talk to God the Father or to Jesus or to the Holy Spirit, about what has happened, responding through your feelings or in words.

God our rock

God is sometimes pictured as a rock, the kind of rock that is solid and strong, gives stability and has permanence (Psalm 62:2). You might have climbed up to a large rock and felt how massive it is beneath your feet. Perhaps you have used stepping stones on the beach or in the countryside to keep your feet dry when crossing a stream or marshy ground, or you have waded through water, not seeing, but feeling, solid ground beneath your feet. God is described as lifting us out of a boggy place and standing us high on a firm foundation (Psalms 27:5; 40:2).

Try one of the following ideas.

Find a rock or large stone. If you can, hold it in your hand. Maybe it is too large to lift. Feel the weight and solidity of it. Look at its colours and surfaces. Feel its texture. What does it tell you about God imaged as a rock?

If somewhere near you there is a rocky place, go there. Sit on or by a rock or a standing stone, paying attention to how it speaks to you of God's faithfulness.

With wax crayons or chalk you could make a rubbing of the surface of a rock, feeling your way into prayer as you do so.

Find a picture of a rock. Prayerfully sit with it, looking at it carefully and then talk to God about what it has told you about him.

Keep your small rock, picture or rubbing in your prayer space, if you have one.

Praying scripture

Find one of the many verses of scripture that speaks to you of God's faithfulness. Here are some suggestions.

> *Who is like you, Lord God Almighty? You, Lord, are mighty, and your faithfulness surrounds you.*
>
> PSALM 89:8, NIV

> *God is faithful who has called you into fellowship with his Son, Jesus Christ our Lord.*
> 1 CORINTHIANS 1:9

Now make your chosen verse your own in one of these ways.

You might read it aloud to yourself, so that you can hear it as well as see it in front of you. Then slowly repeat your chosen verse several times, listening to it and letting it settle into you, as you gradually fall into silence and savour it. Enjoy God's presence through it. Eventually respond to how God has been for you in this time.

Another way would be to memorise it, so that it is always with you as a resource or a prompt, reminding you of God's constancy.

You could also turn a verse into a prayer or statement of what you believe or would like to believe more deeply. For example, 1 Corinthians 1:9 could be adapted to: 'God, I believe that you have called me into fellowship with your son Jesus Christ our Lord. I believe that you are faithful. I believe that you will keep me strong to the end.'

The faithfulness of God's gifting

When we were children, all of us in our family, adults included, enjoyed turning on a lamp in a darkened room and using our hands to make shadow animals on a bare wall. Gradually the wall turned into a menagerie, full of angry wolves, slithering snakes, graceful butterflies or rabbits with long ears. Yet we only had to move or twist our hands and the animals changed into something that had no recognisable shape, or which loomed large and then disappeared altogether. Disappointingly, we could not keep them for another time.

The faithfulness of God

On a day full of sunshine I have watched with pleasure the dappled light as the shadows of leaves and branches move and dance under a tree, or the shadow-shape of a window frame slowly moving across the wall of a room as the hours pass. Then the sun goes in and the shadows are no more. However beautiful they might be, they have no substance or permanence.

James 1:17 describes the faithfulness of God's gifting like this: 'Every good and perfect gift is from above, coming down from the Father of the heavenly lights, who does not change like shifting shadows.'

On a sunny day, enjoy watching shadows move in a park, garden or countryside or on walls of buildings or pavements as people move along. Watch your own shadow lengthen and shorten as you move. Give thanks that, unlike the shadows, God is unchanging, ever faithful.

Alternatively, maybe you would like to make your own shapes with your hands held between a light and a wall in a darkened room. As you turn the light on and the shadows are no more, remember the words of James about God's unchanging, generous giving, which is more trustworthy than any fleeting shadow.

Anchored in the hope of God's faithfulness

The author of the book of Hebrews uses the image of an anchor to help us understand God's faithfulness. The writer reminds us that God kept his promise to Abraham through all Abraham's wanderings and at a time when the fulfilment of the promise of a son and many descendants seemed impossible (Hebrews 6:13–15). Our understanding of God's faithfulness in keeping this promise informs our hope in the faithfulness of God to us. God does not change and can be trusted to keep his promises.

'We have this hope as an anchor for the soul, firm and secure' (Hebrews 6:19). Just as a ship's anchor, tied by a rope, keeps the vessel in place and stops it drifting away on the tide and perhaps being battered to pieces, so our hope in God's promises keeps us where we are safe and prevents us from drifting off course, away from the security of God's purposes for us.

Plait or twist several strands of wool or string together, making the individual strands into a much stronger 'rope'. As you do so, repeatedly say a verse from the Bible that helps you to anchor yourself, or someone for whom you have concern, in God and to hold on to God's promises. You may have a verse that comes to mind. If not, here are some suggestions:

> *'Surely I am with you always, to the very end of the age.'*
> MATTHEW 28:20

> *'Never will I leave you; never will I forsake you.'*
> HEBREWS 13:5

> *'I have loved you with an everlasting love. Therefore I will continue my faithfulness to you.'*
> JEREMIAH 31:3, NRSV

> *'Do not be afraid, little flock, for your Father has been pleased to give you the kingdom.'*
> LUKE 12:32, NIV

> *'Take my yoke upon you and learn from me, for I am gentle and humble in heart, and you will find rest for your souls. For my yoke is easy, and my burden is light.'*
> MATTHEW 11:29–30

You might like to walk or move, make music or dance to the rhythm of the words, or you could clap or use an empty box to drum out the rhythm of the words as you say them.

God as a faithful parent

The prophet Hosea pictures God's faithfulness to Israel (Ephraim) as that of a caring parent with a child (Hosea 11:3–4). He lovingly teaches his child to walk, 'taking them by the arms', patiently supporting and encouraging them. He heals them, 'but they did not realise'. He leads them with 'cords of human kindness, with ties of love' and bends down to feed them. When the child turns away from his parent, and despite his anger at their behaviour, God is full of anguish. 'How can I give you up, Ephraim? How can I hand you over, Israel? … My heart is changed within me; all my compassion is aroused' (v. 8).

Hosea may well have come to a greater understanding of the nature of God's faithfulness through his own experience of being a father or seeing other loving parents nurturing their children. If caring human parents can love, nurture and remain faithful to their children, how much deeper must God's relationship be with his children.

Relax and ask God to be with you in your imagination as you picture a parent encouraging a child to stand and then walk. Let the scene develop as if you were watching a film. How does the parent help the child to stand by itself and precariously balance? What happens when the child sits down suddenly? How do you feel as you see the parent kneeling with hands outstretched, holding the child's hands and drawing it closer with small steps, or walking behind the child holding both its hands? Then comes the moment when the child takes off on his or her own with smiles of delight. Picture the parent's joy. Perhaps the child falls over, picks herself up and tries again. Maybe the parent has to comfort the child before he feels confident enough to walk again, or follow after him later, as he careers off into danger.

How have you seen God in all of this?

What might God be showing you for yourself or for others?

Talk to God about what you have imagined. How might God respond?

God as a faithful, forgiving husband

Hosea's wife, Gomer, was unfaithful to him, but he was willing to reconcile with her and take her back at practical, as well as probably personal, cost to himself (Hosea 3:1–3). Again, in his personal life, Hosea saw a great truth about God. Hosea realised that, as he could forgive his wife, who had been unfaithful to him, how much more God, who is so much greater, wanted to forgive his people, who had been unfaithful in their relationship with him. God woos his people, 'Therefore I am now going to allure her; I will lead her into the wilderness and speak tenderly to her' (2:14). Then there is the beautiful image of God betrothing himself to Israel forever, 'in righteousness and justice, in love and compassion. I will betroth you in faithfulness and you will acknowledge the Lord' (vv. 19–20). God has yearned for his people and acts with gentle determination to bring them back into a loving, faithful, everlasting relationship with him.

How do you feel about the idea of God wooing you into an intimate relationship of betrothal? Tell God about your feelings and thoughts.

Thank God that he remains faithful when we have done wrong in whatever way and is always desiring to take us back into intimate relationship with him.

Pray for:
all those who are having problems with any kind of relationship, personal, at work or within the church;
for all peacemakers and reconcilers;
for counsellors and all who help in the healing of fragmented relationships;
for those who give pastoral care.

You could ground your prayers by clasping a holding cross as you pray.

Try using your body in prayer by lying on the floor with arms outstretched in the shape of a cross.

God our refuge

What does the word 'refuge' mean to you? Maybe you think of a person to whom you can always go when you are tired or in difficulties; someone with whom you find shelter. Perhaps it is a safe place. A traffic island in a busy street can be called a refuge. Pilgrims who walk across the flat sands to the Holy Island of Lindisfarne in Northumberland pass shelters mounted high above them, with ladders to climb up into them if pilgrims are caught by the incoming tide, providing a place where they can wait with some protection for the next low tide. Refugees flee from a place of danger to a place of greater safety.

God is often described as our refuge and a fortress, one in whom we can trust (Psalm 91:2), and as a strong tower that has not failed in providing protection against enemies (61:3). He is a stronghold for all in trouble (9:9) and is called 'my fortress, my God on whom I can rely' (59:9–10).

God is also beautifully pictured as place of shelter in the words 'hide me in the shadow of your wings' (17:8; 36:7; 57:1), as one who covers us with feathers; and whose faithfulness is our shield and rampart (91:4).

Think of the image of God as our refuge. What does this mean for you?

Pray for all refugees and for those who give them help and shelter.

Ponder Psalm 91, which tells of God's faithful protection.

Are there other images of God that speak to you of God's faithfulness? Draw symbols or pictures of them.

Does any particular colour symbolise God's faithfulness to you? Enjoy holding some fabric in that colour or use felt-tip pens or coloured pencils to shade tones of your colour over some paper.

God's faithfulness involves justice

God is faithful in his concern for all people, in his care for the world and its inhabitants. It is part of God's nature. 'A faithful God, who does no wrong, upright and just is he' (Deuteronomy 32:4). Fairness through right living is part of God's justice. Again and again the Bible emphasises that God expects us to care for the marginalised, the orphans, the widows and strangers in the land. A fair and just society is important. 'Hate evil, love good; maintain justice in the courts' (Amos 5:15). Amos has strong words for women (and men) who live comfortably yet treat the poor badly (4:1). He understands God as saying, 'Let justice roll on like a river, righteousness like a never-failing stream' (5:24).

The problems of injustice in today's world might seem too huge for us to solve as individuals, but the way we live can make a difference.

How might you be part of God's unending desire for justice? Here are some ideas from which to choose.

The faithfulness of God

As you read a newspaper, pray for the situations or people featured in it or on the internet, the radio or television news.

Cut or tear headlines and pictures from a newspaper. Prayerfully paste them on some paper in the shape of a cross. Then consider what you have created, giving the situations and people to God.

Go for a prayer walk, giving to God each place, person and situation that you see.

Write to your MP or add your name to an online petition.

Shop fairly and responsibly.

Notice ways in which you can treat God's world with respect and care.

Is there any action or care for others in your locality with which you could help?

There are many organisations working for justice among the poor or marginalised, for peace or for environmental issues. Decide on one or two that you could support in whatever way seems best to you.

A personal response to God's faithfulness

As you look back over this section about the faithfulness of God, what are your thoughts or feelings about this facet of the nature of God? You might like to list them. With discernment, you could bring encouragement to another person by talking about God's faithfulness (Psalm 40:9–10).

Is there anything to which you wish to return, pray through or build into your own pattern of prayer?

Another way of responding is by completing this simple acrostic or by writing your own, using coloured pencils or felt-tip pens.

The faithfulness of God

Faithful One
Always with us
I
T
H
F
U
L

O
N
E

You could respond to God's faithfulness by writing your thoughts in your journal if you have one, or by creating your own poem or honest letter to God, maybe decorated or coloured to express your thoughts or feelings, remembering that in scripture we have the promises that 'I the Lord, do not change' (Malachi 3:6) and that 'Jesus Christ is the same yesterday and today and for ever' (Hebrews 13:8).

24 NOVEMBER–7 DECEMBER

Facing the challenge

Dorinda Miller

Priority

2 Chronicles 20:1–4

While the books of Samuel and Kings tell the story of Israel's kings, the writer of Chronicles looks at the same events from another perspective and with a particular emphasis on the themes of worship and kingship.

We will look at 2 Chronicles 20:1–30 under the headings of priority, prayer, prophecy, prepare, praise and plunder, and consider and reflect together how the message of this chapter can impact our lives and equip us for the challenges that life presents.

I cannot pinpoint exactly when I read this chapter for the first time, but I know it was key to facing the challenge of a deportation order in Asia, shortly after we had arrived to work with the Leprosy Mission. The principles have become, for me, a way of coping with a variety of challenges ever since.

I would like to invite you to read 2 Chronicles 20:1–30 a couple of times in order to gain an overview of the story.

Jehoshaphat's initial reaction to the news that a vast army was coming against him was not to summon his generals, to muster his army, or to collapse in despair. His priority was to resolve to 'enquire of the Lord'.

When we first received the news of the deportation order, so many questions and thoughts raced through our minds! We shared the news with our children before our evening meal, and

Facing the challenge

we prayed together.

Think back to a time when you faced a significant challenge.
What was it?
How did you feel?
What thoughts or fears went through your mind?
How did you respond?
What did you do?
How was the challenge resolved?
How long did it take?
What did you learn through the challenge about yourself, other people and about God?

You may find it helpful to record your answers in your journal, if you have one.

Prayer

2 Chronicles 20:5–13

When it comes to prayer, we can have a wide knowledge and understanding of the subject, but in order to grow and develop our prayer life we have to 'just do it' (to echo the words of a strapline of a sports company). The Bible contains many excellent examples of prayers and, in these verses, Jehoshaphat provides one of them.

Read 2 Chronicles 20:5–13. In his prayer, Jehoshaphat...

- acknowledges the sovereignty and power of God
- remembers how God has assisted them in the past
- recognises the ways in which the people have turned to God
- states the current situation with the imminent invasion from the men of Ammon, Moab, and Mount Seir
- recognises that he does not know what to do
- looks to God for wisdom and direction

In some ways Jehoshaphat's prayer echoes Paul's advice to the Philippians, 'The Lord is near. Do not be anxious about anything, but in every situation, by prayer and petition, with thanksgiving, present your requests to God' (Philippians 4:5–6).

Reflect on your current circumstances or on those of someone close to you, and write your own prayer using the model Jehoshaphat uses in these verses, outlined above.

The night before my husband went to the meeting where he was informed he was under a deportation order and his passport was taken from him, sleep was elusive! As I prayed, I was reminded about Moses holding up his stick and the Red Sea parting, so that the Israelites could pass safely to the other side. I also prayed that God would prompt our friends to pray for us as we faced this challenge, since we did not have a telephone, and communicating with those around us and in the UK was a challenge in itself, in those days before the internet was widely available! The next morning, as I waited with my children for their school bus, a rickshaw drew up and a Finnish friend got out. When the bus had gone, she came up to our flat and explained why she had come. She had felt that we were facing trouble and wanted to pray for us, and God had also given her a word for us—when the Israelites left Egypt, they saw the Egyptians coming after them, but Moses lifted up his stick and the Red Sea parted for them. It was a great encouragement and strengthened us for the difficulties that lay ahead as we waited for the order to be overturned.

Prophecy

2 Chronicles 20:14–17

As all the people waited on God, the Spirit of the Lord fell on Jahaziel, and he spoke God's words to the assembly, which

Facing the challenge

provided the people with encouragement and clear directions about what to do, where to go and what to expect.

Read verses 14–17 and reflect on them. Imagine the scene, the vast assembly, the sense of urgency and expectancy. Watch Jahaziel as he speaks; how do you feel as you hear his words? How do you want to respond to them? Join in the worship and praise. Ask God for wisdom and guidance on any difficulties that you, or someone known to you, are currently facing.

Sometimes we receive clear instructions from God on how to navigate situations, and yet at other times, the guidance seems to come bit by bit as we continue to put our hand in his and keep walking in faith.

In terms of the deportation challenge, after the initial encouragement of the verses in Exodus 14, we continued to receive at intervals encouragement to stand firm and wait for God to resolve the situation. One particular day I had a strong sense that I should pray that one of our Asian friends, who knew about the situation we were facing, would have dinner with his uncle. So I prayed that he would. When my husband came home he asked me to guess who this friend was having dinner with that evening, and I replied: his uncle. My husband was surprised and asked if I knew who his uncle was. I had no idea. He told me that the uncle was a very senior government minister!

Prepare

2 Chronicles 20:20–21

These verses tell us that the Israelites left early in the morning but do not mention the preparations for departure. This may well be a testimony to their state of preparedness given the times that they were living in and their need to be ready to defend themselves.

Facing the challenge

Soon we will be entering the season of Advent and moving towards celebrating Christmas. So today we will take time out from the story in 2 Chronicles to consider how we can prepare for these seasons in a way that is appropriate for us as individuals in the circumstances in which we currently find ourselves.

I suggest that you begin by reflecting on how you have journeyed through this season in the past.

What have you enjoyed and appreciated about Advent?

How have you used this time devotionally, to prepare for Christmas?

What have you found difficult?

How have you encountered God during this season?

How has God broken into your busyness and routines during Advent to show you fresh signs of his love and forgiveness?

You may like to make a note of your responses in your journal, if you have one.

In the light of your responses about previous seasons of Advent, how would you like to mark the season this year, and what strategies or activities can you put in place to achieve these?

Are there any creative activities you can engage in during this season?

Take some time to be still and lay out your proposed Advent activities, actions, strategies and ideas before God and listen for his perspective on them. Then gather the resources you require and be ready to start when Advent commences!

Praise

2 Chronicles 20:18–19, 22, 26, 28

There is a strong theme of praise and worship in this passage, which shows how God's powerful intervention can be released, as the focus moves from the situation facing them to God. This is clearly demonstrated again in the New Testament, in Acts 16, where Paul and Silas find themselves in prison, having been whipped and beaten. Instead of focusing on their circumstances and injuries, they are praising God, and as they do so, there is an earthquake that shakes the prison and frees them from their chains. As a result, the jailer and his entire household become believers.

Across denominations there are wide variations in the way people praise and worship God. Spend a few minutes reflecting on the ways in which you have experienced praise and worship within your own journey of faith. Think about what you enjoy about praise and worship. What do you find difficult? How does God meet you personally at those times? Finally, spend some time in praise and worship.

One late Friday afternoon my daughter and I were returning home on a rickshaw when she suddenly and spontaneously began to sing the chorus from a song we had sung in church earlier in the day. The words were, 'And to God be the glory, and to God be the glory, for this is the gospel of Christ.' I joined in with her and, much to the astonishment and amusement of the rickshaw driver, we sang all the way home! However, by the time we arrived home, this chorus had taken root within me and I continued to sing it silently all evening and much of the night. We discovered some weeks later that the order had been overturned and signed on the Saturday morning. Many months later, on a trip home to the UK, we heard from a close friend who had been supporting us in prayer that she had stopped praying about the deportation order on the Friday evening, when she had felt God saying, 'It is done.' Although the order was overturned, it then took a further couple of months to obtain the security clearance, work permit and visas. These finally arrived at 5 pm one Sunday, just in time for us to go to the evening service at church, to share

Plunder

2 Chronicles 20:24–25

By the time Jehoshaphat and his army arrived at the battle site, there were only dead bodies, and so they set about gathering the plunder. The word 'plunder' is traditionally defined as stealing goods from someone or somewhere, and generally implies that these goods are taken by violence and dishonesty. In this instance, the Ammonites and Moabites and men from Mount Seir had annihilated each other, so Jehoshaphat and his men did not have to fight or take anything by force. Instead, it took them three days to collect the plunder—a great quantity of equipment and clothing and items of value—before returning joyfully to Jerusalem.

What an amazing answer to prayer! Seeking God for guidance and following God's directions not only provided a great deliverance, but also the gift of a vast quantity of plunder. This was an unexpected gift and an abundant blessing.

Reversing the deportation order was an amazing answer to prayer and a testimony to God's divine intervention in the circumstances. At that time, people who were issued with deportation orders always went, if not within a few days, then within a few weeks. God enabled us to stay for our full two-year assignment.

Read Psalm 136, which charts God's goodness to the Israelites. Then write your own version, using events from your own journey of faith that chart God's love, goodness and provision for you. Or you may prefer to do this pictorially through painting or drawing the events in your journey.

Facing the challenge

A for adore

While the calendar year starts in January and the tax year in April, the church year starts in November with the season of Advent. It begins on the Sunday nearest to 30 November (St Andrew's Day) and continues until Christmas Eve. It is a time of preparation as we wait in anticipation for the king to come. It is a time not only to prepare and look forward to the birth of Jesus, but also a time of anticipation, as we acknowledge that the day will come when Jesus once again returns to earth.

Last week offered an opportunity to reflect on how you had used this season previously, and also to consider how you might enter into it afresh this year. As you begin to carry out what you planned, may 'the Lord bless you and keep you; the Lord make his face shine upon you and be gracious to you; the Lord turn his face towards you and give you peace' (Numbers 6:24–26).

To begin the season of Advent we will look at six themes, each one based on a letter in the word Advent—A for adore, D for desire, V for vine, E for everlasting, N for new and T for travel.

Dictionaries offer two definitions of the word 'adore': firstly to regard with the utmost esteem, respect, honour, affection and love, and secondly to worship and to pay divine honour.

At Christmas we usually join together in singing the carol, 'O come all ye faithful' with its chorus that invites us to 'come, let us adore him'. What does this mean to you? How do you seek to adore God, not only in this season but throughout the year? When you have reflected on these questions, see if you can listen to one of the songs listed below (both of which are available on iTunes), or another song of adoration:

'Adoramus te Domine' (We adore you, O Lord) from the Taizé Community. This can be found on a number of their recordings, for example *Cantate* and *Laudate*.

'Adore Him', Track 7 on *My Soul Yearns* CD, Vineyard Records UK 2011.

D is for desire

Let us consider what the desires of our own hearts are at this time. How do they line up with God's word and will for our lives?

Read the verses below from Psalm 37 three times and choose a word, phrase or sentence to meditate on for a few minutes.

Trust in the Lord and do good: dwell in the land and enjoy safe pasture.
Take delight in the Lord and he will give you the desires of your heart.
Commit your way to the Lord;
Trust in him and he will do this...
Be still before the Lord and wait patiently for him.

PSALM 37:3–5, 7

V for vine

I'd like to invite you today to come on a journey. You have been invited to see the oldest vine in the country, which is growing in a conservatory at a large, old country house. This is a special day, as you have a private invitation and the general public do not usually have access to this vine. How do you feel about this invitation? Excited? Not bothered? Perplexed as to how you got the invitation?

Imagine arriving at the estate and driving up the mile-long drive. Take time to notice as many details as you can: the weather, the scenery, the house as it comes into view. As you draw near the house, an elderly man comes out to greet you. Observe him carefully. What is he like? What is he wearing? How does he walk? What strikes you about his face? You get out of the car and greet him. He warmly shakes your hand and welcomes you and takes you round to the back of the house and through the gardens towards the conservatory. What do you talk about? What do you notice about the gardens?

You arrive at the conservatory and he opens the door. You go in. The vine is massive and the old man begins to tell you its history. You see the old gnarled trunk, the branches spreading out, and the leaves. What are you thinking? What are you feeling? You see where the vine has been pruned and trimmed over the years and the abundant growth that has resulted from such care. It is quiet and peaceful in the conservatory, and the old man says that he will leave you for a while to enjoy the peace and the vine.

As you are looking at the vine, you hear someone call your name. You turn round and there is Jesus. What does he say to you? What do you want to say to him? Are there any parts of your life that he wants to prune? Will you let him do so? Are there any questions you have for him about your own growth and fruitfulness? Spend time with him. Before he leaves, Jesus cuts off a bunch of grapes and gives it to you. Once he has gone, you leave the conservatory and sit on the old wooden garden bench outside. You enjoy the warmth of the sunshine, the view of the gardens and house, and the grapes.

Then, when you are ready, slowly return to the room. You may like to record your experience of this meditation in your journal.

E for everlasting

While change is an inevitable part of life, the pace of change has increased in recent years, especially within the field of technology. To think that at the beginning of this millennium there was, for example, no Facebook or Twitter, and now there are a number of ways of connecting with people who are both near and far.

Against this backdrop of cultural and global change we read in the Old Testament, 'I the Lord do not change' (Malachi 3:6), and in the New Testament we read that 'Jesus Christ is the same yesterday and today and for ever'(Hebrews 13:8).

In our consumer society there is little that is truly everlasting—things are no longer made to last! However, in the Bible there are many references to everlasting—approximately 67 in the Old Testament and 26 in the New Testament.

The Bible mentions everlasting
- … mercy (Psalm 100:5, KJ21)
- … righteousness (Psalm 119:142)
- … joy (Isaiah 35:10)
- … kindness (Isaiah 54:8)
- … light (Isaiah 60:19),
- … life (Daniel 12:2 and John 3:16, KJ21).

Take time to reflect on what the Bible says is everlasting. How does this impact your journey of faith?

Finally, choose one of the verses below, to take with you and mull over at intervals during the day.

> *Whenever the rainbow appears in the clouds, I will see it and remember the everlasting covenant between God and all living creatures of every kind on the earth.*
> GENESIS 9:16

> *But from everlasting to everlasting the Lord's love is with those who fear him.*
> PSALM 103:17

> *He is the Everlasting Father, the Prince of Peace.*
> ISAIAH 9:6

N for new

> *'I will give you a new heart and put a new spirit in you; I will remove from you your heart of stone and give you a heart of flesh.'*
> EZEKIEL 36:26

As we journey through Advent, looking forward with expectation to Christmas, there is an opportunity for us 'to reflect on the reason for the season. Advent is a time to prepare our hearts for Christ, just as we prepare our homes for Christmas' (J. John, *A Christmas Compendium*, Philo Trust 2012, p. 9).

We looked at the desires of our hearts earlier; today our focus is on the state of our hearts and their need for renovation. There is no quick, easy or instant technique to achieve the renovation required. Rather, it is through openness to God, in silence and solitude, in the midst of the busyness of our daily lives, that God works, as we journey through the challenges, the joys and sorrows that life brings us.

Take a piece of A4 paper and fold it in half widthways. Then draw a heart shape on each half of the page—just the shape; no anatomical drawing skills needed! Write 'heart of stone' under one shape and 'heart of flesh' under the other. Consider what areas of your heart are hard and stony, and jot these down on the appropriate heart shape. Then repeat the process with the other heart and consider which areas are soft and flesh-like. When you have finished, spend some time meditating on the above verse from Ezekiel and listen to what the Lord wants to reveal to you through it.

T for travel

As we read through the Bible, we see that travel is a recurring theme, from Abraham leaving Ur and setting out to travel to Canaan, to the children of Israel leaving Egypt to travel to the promised land, to Jesus travelling around spreading the news of the kingdom of God, to Paul and his missionary journeys, which took him further afield and into other countries. Travel features prominently in the Christmas story, too: Mary and Joseph travel to Bethlehem; the shepherds follow the angels' advice to go to Bethlehem, and the kings travel from afar to see the newborn king.

In our day and age many people travel during the Christmas season to visit family and friends. How do you feel about the journeys you will make over the coming weeks? Although this time is traditionally viewed as one of peace and goodwill as we prepare for, and then celebrate the birth of Jesus, for many people it can be fraught with busyness and stress. Thank God that he knows your situation and the people involved intimately, whether they know him or not. Lay before him your hopes and fears, listen to his perspective, and seek his wisdom and insight. Imagine the preparations and celebrations and ask him how he may want to use you as a channel of his everlasting love, light, life and kindness.

Finally, sit in a comfortable upright position and close your eyes. In the quiet, imagine that you are breathing in God's peace and love and life, and breathing out any worry, anxiety or concerns that you may have. Continue with this for five to ten minutes.

Ask God where he is calling you to go this Advent season, and what steps you can take to follow him.

8–21 DECEMBER

Announcing good news

Anne Noble

Good news in Advent

Advent is a time of year for thinking about both the inward and the outward journey of transformation. During what is traditionally a penitential season in the Church, we look inward to the places where we ourselves need to be changed. We seek forgiveness for wrongs done and rights not done, and we can also challenge our thinking and doing—drawing us closer to the time when we both remember and look forward to the advent (coming) of Jesus. Advent is good news for individuals because it is a time of reflection on how our lives can be transformed by the life of God.

Advent is also good news for the world. The outward journey is about lifting our heads to the vision of a new heaven and a new earth, one in which God reigns and the world is transformed. It is a time of recognising that another world, God's kingdom, is both possible and is coming and that we can work towards this now.

The readings for this section reflect both these themes of personal and community transformation and represent good news for each of us and for the communities in which we live, both in the present moment and in the hoped-for future when Christ will return.

Opening reflection

Find a quiet space and settle into silence. Reflect on the day that has been (or yesterday if this is the morning). What was good and life-giving about it? Spend some time thinking about these things. Give thanks to God for these moments of your day. Now turn to anything that might have disturbed you, which you found challenging or difficult. Were there situations that felt broken? Hold these things one by one before God and imagine him transforming them into something life-giving.

Anointing

Isaiah 61:1–11

This passage from Isaiah is written to a people returning from exile in Babylon to the remains of the city of Jerusalem and the remnant of the people of God there. Yet all is not fully restored, and so this passage points forward to a new time and a new vision in which individuals and community are renewed. The passage begins with the anointing of the Lord's servant; notice that this anointing is not for himself but to benefit the people of God. Read verses 1–4 slowly, pausing to notice all those places and people to whom the Lord's anointed is to minister. On a piece of paper write these down. Are any of these you at this time?

Now read the verses again and notice the repeated word 'instead': 'a crown of beauty instead of ashes, the oil of joy instead of mourning and a garment of praise instead of a spirit of despair' (v. 4). All this is so that those ministered to can rebuild and repair—the people are built up by the servant so that they can rebuild their community.

Pause at this point and pray for your own building up. Now call to mind the communities in which you live or work. Where is there brokenness, devastation or ruin? How might God be calling you to build up places or people? If you keep a journal, this might be a place to write down those people, relationships and places for which you have prayed.

Prayer

Lord God, your spirit rests upon your people today and leads us to those in need. Anoint me with your spirit this day, that in the places I walk where there is oppression, broken-heartedness, grief, and captivity I may both proclaim and be good news.

Light in darkness

The symbol for Amnesty International is a candle wrapped in barbed wire. In one of the chapels I like to visit, just such a candle burns day and night. It is a symbol of defiant hope and a reminder to pray for those who are prisoners of conscience throughout the world. Isaiah 61:1 speaks of freedom for captives and release from darkness for prisoners. The exiles who have been held captive in Babylon are now to be free, and light is to come to those in prison.

What kinds of prisons hold people in darkness? These might be literal prisons in some places in the world, or they could be matters of circumstance, ill health, poverty and other social issues that have become jails for many.

In your home, create a space to use as a prayer focus for the next two weeks. As we read through the passages of Advent, we will gradually add to what is there. To begin, place a candle in the space. You might like to place some prickly branches around it, if you have access to some. (Be careful that they cannot catch the flame.) Re-read Isaiah 61:1–4. Call to mind the dark places of this world, or even your own life. Now light the candle.

I light this candle as a reminder that your light, O Creator, shines in the darkness—it brings life from chaos and the void.
I light this candle as a reminder that your light, O Redeemer, can never be extinguished—it heals and restores places where life is broken.
I light this candle, sustaining Spirit, as a prayer of defiant hope that wherever there is darkness your light may shine in power to strengthen and encourage.
Creator, redeemer and sustainer of all life—shine hope and life into the darkness today.
Amen

Praying with the news

Isaiah 61:1–4

Take a selection of magazines and newspapers, local, national and international. Look through them and identify the oppressed, broken-hearted, captive and grieving. Do not limit your identification of captives to those in literal prisons, but think also of those imprisoned by circumstances such as illness or poverty. Use one of these ideas to pray for these individuals.

Prayer board

Make a prayer board or collage from the cuttings. Place it where you will see it every day, or in a prayer corner if you have one, along with the words of Isaiah 61:1–2. As you pray for the people and situations in the news, say the words of the verses slowly as a prayer for them.

Oil and tears

On a table, place two small bowls. Fill one with olive oil and the other with salt water (to represent tears). As you dip your fingers in the water, hold before God those who mourn all kinds of losses (bereavement, jobs, dignity, health, peace, and so on). Remember to include yourself if appropriate. Now dip your fingers in the oil and pray for God to pour out the oil of gladness, healing and life on those you hold before him.

Crowns, oil and garments

Take some of your newspaper articles, and as you hold the stories and circumstances described there before God, cut out crown, bottle or garment shapes from them. As you do so, pray the words: 'A crown of beauty instead of ashes; the oil of joy instead of mourning; and a garment of praise instead of a spirit of despair' (Isaiah 61:3). If you have a Christmas tree, you might like to turn these into alternative decorations.

A liturgy of preciousness

The images in verses 7–11 particularly are a picture of beauty. Among the images are those that speak of a new and honoured beginning for the people of God. Instead of devastation and ruins, defeat and exile, shame and disgrace, robbery and wrongdoing, there will be new buildings, joy, a future, justice and blessing. Some of the images apply to the community of the people of Israel; others appear to apply to individuals. These are images of restoration for individuals and nations as a sign of hope to the world.

In your quiet space, use the following liturgy to help you apply these words to yourself and to your community. You might like to write them out on a card and take them with you as you travel in your community, praying them in places in your neighbourhood that need hope and restoration. Add a copy to your prayer corner.

In the ruined places of life God speaks of new creation

Lord, come, bring restoration and hope.

Where there has been pain for time out of mind

Lord, come, bring restoration and hope.

In torn places of shame and disgrace

Lord, come, bring restoration and hope.

In places where the future feels empty

Lord, come, bring restoration and hope.

In places of injustice

Lord, come, bring restoration and hope.

Lord, cover us with your beauty, adorn us with your love, and grow us into your people—a sign of your presence for restoration and hope.

Beginning again

The people for whom Isaiah writes were returning from exile in Babylon. During the time that they were away, their city and their land had fallen to ruin and neglect, and now the significant task of rebuilding and renewal would begin for them. Though they were returning to all that they had missed, nothing would be the same. The land and Jerusalem were different, and exile would have changed the people as well. I imagine that amid the joy of return there might have been disappointment that nothing was as it had been preserved in their collective memories, and there would be concern about the amount of work that lay ahead. Perhaps they might have wondered what God was bringing them back to. Did 'home' feel like 'home' any more, especially to a generation born in exile?

God promises that the rebuilding will happen and his people will once again be recognised among the nations as blessed by the Lord—but these things take time and do not happen overnight. At the end of this passage, in Isaiah 61:11, the prophet brings words of hope, 'the soil makes the young plant come up and a garden causes seeds to grow'. As any gardener knows, growth can be a slow process. I once grew a plant that took years before it flowered. Year after year I looked after it, and each year I wondered whether it was worth keeping going, but eventually, after four years, it produced the most beautiful and delicate flowers. The promise God makes here is that good soil and gardens will produce growth—even if it is a long time before anything is visible. In our lives too, the good soil of faith will produce growth, even though sometimes it feels like a hard slog to keep going.

Prayer

Heavenly Father, when nothing seems to be happening and the familiar patterns of life no longer carry the same feeling of your presence, help me to be patient and to find peace in believing that you are at work, bringing slow growth in the soil of my faith.

Announcing good news

God's messengers

Luke 1:26–38

This Bible passage tells of the angel Gabriel's message to Mary that she will be the mother of God's Son, who will be king and saviour. The words may be so familiar that we have lost the impact of their meaning and the depth of courage of Mary's response.

Take a moment to read the passage slowly. Now read it again. As you do so, imagine that you are Gabriel charged by God to speak to a teenage girl who is just on the edge of married life in a small town in Galilee. You know the significance of the message you are about to bring to the world, and you know how highly God regards this girl. You also know she will be startled and probably frightened by your appearance. Spend some time reflecting on Gabriel's role in this passage.

Angels are God's messengers. What message do you want to hear from God?

Read the passage again. This time imagine that you are Mary. Remember that she is a young girl in her early teens as you do so. What do you see as the angel appears? Hear the angel's words and imagine that they are spoken to you. What impact do these words have on you? How do you feel?

None of us will be called to the same path as Mary, yet each of us lives a called life as a Christian. Spend some time reflecting on what God has called you to in life. This doesn't have to be a specific church ministry; it could be your job, a role in your family, or he may ask you to use a particular gift he has given you. You may like to record your thoughts in your journal if you use one. Remember, God is not bound by the conventions of this world; he can choose and call surprising people to do extraordinary things and others simply to live ordinary lives that nevertheless speak of him.

Announcing good news

As you hold your calling before God, you may find the following prayer helpful.

God of life, you call me to a life that I alone can live. Strengthen me by your Spirit, that I may live in all the fullness you long for me to know, so that others may see that you live in me and I in you.

Creating space for the holy

The angel Gabriel comes to Mary in her home town, amid the ordinary things of her life. Mary was engaged to be married and no doubt could see what her future looked like in the lives of the other married women and mothers of Nazareth.

God's messenger comes into her ordinary working space and makes it a holy place. Mary, in her profound acceptance of God's call, creates a holy space within her life for the Son of God.

In your home, find a quiet space in a place where you normally work (perhaps in the kitchen or study)—maybe somewhere you don't normally pray. Settle and still yourself. You may well find this difficult, as no doubt around you are many distractions— jobs waiting to be done, things left undone. Try to let go of them one by one. I find it helpful to have a note book in which I can write down a list of the things that distract me, but you may be able simply to call them to mind and then to put them down before God. It may be that in doing this you recognise his promptings in the ordinary tasks and objects around you.

Re-read Luke 1:26–38 slowly. Imagine God entering the space in which you are now sitting. What is the message he has for you? What would you want to say to him? What feels impossible in your life at the present time? Remember that God calls the most unexpected of people to great things. On our own the things he asks of us may seem impossible—caring for those who are sick, grieving with those who mourn, forgiving those who have hurt us, working alongside those we find challenging, sharing his good news with those who seem not to care and who mock us for it. But God does not leave us on our own; as with Mary, he fills us with his Holy Spirit so that what feels impossible for us becomes possible in the mysterious presence of his power.

Pray that you might experience God's presence. Remain in quiet for as long as you are able.

Prayer

Extraordinary God, vast and beautiful beyond our imaginings, fill our everyday lives with your presence and transform them with your glory.

Posada

There is an old Mexican tradition in which young people dressed as Mary and Joseph travel from house to house in their communities during the weeks before Christmas. Wherever they stop, they ask for a room for the night and tell the story of the imminent arrival of Jesus. Today some churches continue the tradition by taking figures of Mary and Joseph from house to house in their parishes. At each house families are encouraged to make room for the holy family and re-read the story of the first Christmas. On Christmas Eve the figures are returned to church to celebrate the birth of Jesus.

In our house we do something similar to mark the days in Advent, using our nativity figures. We place the empty stable in a central position and then the figures of Mary and Joseph, the shepherds and the magi in different places throughout the house. The angels are moved between the figures, depending upon which part of the Christmas story we are thinking about that day.

As Christmas approaches, the figures converge on the stable (except of course for the magi, who wait for the feast of Epiphany). On Christmas Eve night we finally place the figure of Jesus in the stable as we return from the midnight service. In this way, we mark the journey of Advent as slowly as we can and allow the story and the journey to fill as much of the house as possible. Eventually all focuses in on Jesus, the son of God born into all our lives.

Why not consider doing something similar this year? If you don't have a nativity set, some simple pictures or words would do just as well. At each place where the figures stay, you could write out a verse from either the Isaiah passage we have read or the annunciation, and leave it as a marker to help you focus on your own journey of transformation this Advent.

The art of the annunciation

If you have access to the internet, search for an image of the painting 'The annunciation' by Henry Ossawa Tanner (1898). If you don't have access to the internet, you could use any picture of the annunciation and adapt the questions below as necessary, or use one of the suggestions at the end.

I find that sometimes I pray better with pictures and art than I can with words. As you approach the painting, try not to come with too many ideas of your own, but simply pray that God will speak to you through the art. The following approach may help.

Once you have the image in front of you, spend some time

simply looking at it. What do you notice? What seems to speak to you? What are the dominant colours and mood of the work?

The painting is unusual in that the angel is not personified but represented by a brilliant blurred line in the painting. Does this remind you of anything? Might it be like a door? Do you see how the dominant lines are horizontals and verticals? How does Mary fit into this? Can you see a cross in the picture, which hints at the future for Jesus?

What is Mary's house like? Do you think this is a physically rich place? How about spiritual wealth?

How does Mary seem to you? Frightened, at peace, tense, questioning, resigned, happy, thoughtful, or something else?

Read Luke 1:26–38 and return to looking at the painting. Does anything new strike you?

Stay with the picture for as long as you need to. If you have a printer, you could print out a copy. If you have created a prayer corner, place the picture there. Does it make a difference to how you see your earlier prayers to place this picture with them? Pray again for these places and situations, that God's presence might transform them.

Prayer

Holy God, you unlock moments in life when a door is opened so that we can see into the life of heaven. Often you beckon us in those moments to come to the threshold, take your hand and cross with you into newness. May your Spirit give us courage to accept the invitation to walk with you into a transformed life.

You could try the following instead:

Drawing the annunciation: through the ages, many artists have tried to paint what this moment of encounter between Mary and the angel was like. If you enjoy drawing, draw your own picture of this moment. If you are confident enough to do this, place your picture somewhere where you will see it as you move around your home.

Writing the annunciation: re-read the passage and take some time in quiet reflection on the words. Now write your own poem or prayer in response to it.

Paying attention: a liturgy

In the annunciation God's attention is focused on Mary, a humble young woman from a poor family with nothing to mark her out from the girl next door, who is nevertheless chosen by God and greeted as the privileged, favoured one. When God chose to break into human history with the gift of salvation, he could have chosen a woman of royal birth; he might have looked for someone in Jerusalem, but instead he went to a village in Galilee called Nazareth to a virgin named Mary engaged to a man named Joseph. At Christmas we are reminded of the truth that God turns his attention to the whole world and to each one of us as named individuals, whoever we are.

Draw around your hands and write your name on the palms of the drawn hand shapes. Cut the shapes out and place them in the prayer space you have created. Use the following liturgy to help you remember that God also focuses his attention on you as an individual and calls you into his service.

Heavenly Father, enthroned in the splendour of heaven,
you hold all that is and has been in your hands,

And you also hold me.

Announcing good news

Lord Jesus Christ, you stretched out your arms on the cross for the sake of the whole world, once for all for all humankind,

And you also stretch out your arms to save me.

Holy Spirit, you hovered over the chaos of dawning time, drawing out all the goodness of creation, and at Pentecost empowered frightened disciples to speak of you,

And you also draw out my potential and empower me.

Father, Son and Holy Spirit, hold me, save me and empower me to use my hands to serve you. May I be your 'yes' to the world.
Amen

Christmas decorations

Select strips of paper (anything reasonably sturdy will do) to create a paper chain. You might like to write on the strips the names of the people, places or situations you have prayed for during Advent. Join the strips together to make a paper chain.

Place your chain in your prayer corner or somewhere else in your home. You could use it as a Christmas decoration.

On Christmas Eve or Christmas Day, try to find a moment when everything is quiet and sit, holding the paper chain in your hand. Remember that Jesus was born into the world to show us how to live lives for God and to free us from the chains that stop us living life to its full. These are some of the situations we have reflected on in our time with Isaiah and Mary, and this is the good news that God's kingdom will be a transformed world.

When you are ready, take the paper chain and break it. As you do so, pray that God's power will once again break into the world and transform it.

22 DECEMBER–4 JANUARY

Forgotten feasts of Christmas

Liz Hoare

St Stephen

Feast day 26 December

There are four special commemorations following Christmas Day that are easily forgotten, even by church leaders. They offer a journey back to Christmas, giving us a chance to ponder the meaning of the season from a different direction and perspective—an approach 'by another way'.

Read Acts 7:44–60. Thinking about the death of the first Christian martyr the day after the birth of the saviour may seem out of kilter, but only if we do not acknowledge life's realities.

Stephen shares his special day with Boxing Day, the day after Christmas, when many of us are sated with food and presents. As Christian tradition developed, St Stephen's Day became a festive day when the poor were sought out and gifts given to them. Masters turned servants and waited on those who normally served them. On this day, servants and apprentices broke open the boxes in which they had collected their tips and shared the money out amongst themselves, hence the name 'Boxing Day'.

One of the few mentions Stephen receives is in the carol 'Good King Wenceslas looked out/On the feast of Stephen'. The final verse goes:

Therefore Christians all, be sure
Wealth or rank possessing,
Ye who now will bless the poor,
Shall yourselves find blessing.

On the day after Christmas Day we may realise the chaos that Christmas brings to normal routine. Whatever the reality of the day after, this is where we will find God at work. After all, Stephen's own story emerges from a row in the early church.

Stephen was one of the first seven deacons, chosen to distribute food among two ethnic groups of widows who were supported by the early church and who were in dispute. These men were to be 'of good standing, full of the Spirit and of wisdom' (6:3). For such attributes to be demanded of people whose primary task was to serve is worth pondering.

Stephen was singled out from the start as a man 'full of faith and the Holy Spirit' (v. 5). He was the only one whose attributes were noted by the author of Acts.

Courage and forgiveness

Stephen's character and deeds brought him to the attention of enemies of the first Christians, and he was brought to trial and condemned to death by stoning. In Acts 7 Luke records his defence, which is an eloquent account of God's acts in history leading up to the coming of the promised messiah. He accused his hearers of opposing the Holy Spirit and, full of rage, they turned on him in violence. Like his Lord, Stephen was an innocent victim, and there are echoes in his dying of Jesus' own death. Like his Lord, he forgave his executioners. In many paintings and stained-glass windows he is depicted dressed as a deacon with his garment held up full of stones. In Denmark people call his day the 'Second Christmas Day', and people go to church to celebrate Christmas in the atmosphere of the first martyr of the faith.

Stephen was the first martyr or 'witness' in the early church. He was a true servant. All he did was to challenge the religious leaders of his day—as indeed Jesus himself had done, with the same results. In both cases this was considered blasphemy.

If we are members of Christ's Church, are we prepared to let him challenge us?

You may like to read Mary's 'Magnificat' (Luke 1:46–55) and pray for the church to have the courage to speak out at the right time, as well as remaining humble enough to hear the challenge to serve and bear witness.

The face of an angel

When Stephen began his defence, everyone who looked at him saw that his face was 'like the face of an angel' (Acts 6:15).

What does that image suggest to you? Have you ever seen anyone radiant like this?

As Stephen died with stones raining down on him, he looked up to heaven and cried, 'Look, I see the heaven opened and the Son of Man standing at the right hand of God' (7:56). Stephen is closely associated with his Lord and saviour in so many respects.

Find a photograph of yourself and also some Christmas cards with angels depicted on them. Look at the cards and then at your own face. Which is more real, more likely to suggest the reality of God to those you love and serve day by day? You may not feel very angelic, but Stephen's story links up angelic ministry with real flesh and blood, and that is where we begin and end.

Read 2 Corinthians 3:18 slowly and prayerfully. You may like to imagine Jesus looking at you. As you look back at him in love, see his reflection grow in your face.

The 19th century Lutheran hymn writer Frederik Hammerich (1809–77) wrote a hymn that linked Stephen with the Bethlehem scene. (In Greek 'stephanos' means 'wreath'—a symbol of victory.)

> *Hail, little child, laid in a crib*
> *Prince of Christmas, yet our*
> *Reconciler with God!*
> *To you belong all praise and might,*
> *The crown of heaven and of all life.*
> *How radiates today with special splendour*
> *Over your crib that wreath*
> *With which your martyr Stephen is adorned,*
> *Because you took him suddenly*
> *Away from us!*
>
> *The peace of the Christmas angels*
> *Comes down upon the eyes*
> *Of the glorified Stephen,*
> *And the power and glory of Christmas*
> *Are revealed in his death.*
> *So he fell into a sweet heavenly sleep*
> *On his bed of stones, unharmed,*
> *Like a babe in his mother's arms.*

Pray for all who serve in the name of Jesus without counting the cost.

The Holy Innocents

Feast day 28 December

There is pain, bleeding and crying at the very heart of Christmas. No birth takes place without them. But the carnage of the massacre of the children of Bethlehem, 'all the boys... who were two years old and under' (Matthew 2:16) is an outrage. Whether it was 20 or the 14,000 of medieval calculations, the murder of these children by a cruel and paranoid ruler brought grief and suffering that cannot be described as anything other than barbarous.

Calling these Bethlehem babies 'holy innocents' may not be the best way to grasp the reality of brutality that exists in the world now as it did then. Herod was a puppet of the Romans, a cruel man in a cruel world. He was so cruel that he had some of his own children killed to make his throne more secure. When the wise men failed to return as they had promised, Herod flew into a rage and ordered the killing of all babies under two in Bethlehem.

The feast day dates back to the fourth or fifth century, but the need to go on remembering the victims of cruelty, whether of the sword, bomb or famine, continues even as we read these words. What can we say or do except remember them? It is not good enough to settle for the sentiment of the collect for this day in the Book of Common Prayer which claims that the holy innocents glorify God by their deaths. That lets us off the hook too easily—and is it true?

There are other children in the Gospel stories, and we know that Jesus placed great value on them. He warned that it was better to be thrown into the sea with a millstone around the neck than to cause just one of these little ones to stumble (Luke 17:2), and he was clear that if we want to know what it means to inhabit the kingdom of God we need to look at a child (Luke 18:16–17). It is their vulnerability and dependence that brings us up short every time and should make us appalled when they suffer.

A Christmas for grown-ups

We are forever tempted to distance ourselves from the meaning of Christmas by saying, 'It's for the children.' Of course it is, and children have their own integrity—but it is also for adults, and we are not doing ourselves or our children any favours by sentimentalising it.

We probably don't want to think about the massacre at Bethlehem in the midst of Christmas cheer, but the feast is there to confront us for our good.

What response can we make to the fact we have just celebrated 'Emmanuel, God with us' in the face of this kind of suffering and evil?

In the birth of Jesus we come face to face with a God who is not simply a distant spectator of such pain, but who, in the cross that overshadows the crib, has actually participated in it.

In Christ, God has shared the world's suffering and faced it head on. The only way we can respond is by seeing the world through his eyes, acknowledging the shame of being part of the humanity that is capable of inflicting such pain on others, resisting quick answers in the face of mystery and affirming that Jesus Christ is Lord even in the midst of suffering, grief and pain.

Pray for refugees everywhere. Find an image online or in the newspaper of people fleeing their homeland. Imagine walking with these people for a while. How does it feel? What is your prayer?

Alternatively, sit quietly for a time and imagine being told to leave your home with only what you can carry. What would you take? How does it feel to leave the rest behind and set off to an unknown destination? Talk to God about those who are doing this right now.

Joy and pain together

Matthew's account of Herod's brutal action is linked to an Old Testament description in the book of Jeremiah of Rachel weeping inconsolably for her butchered children when Jerusalem fell to the Babylonians (see Jeremiah 31:15–17).

It may seem strange to think of tears as a spiritual gift, but they have been regarded as such at different times in the church's history. Tears are a neglected gift even though, at this time of year especially, many people will be acutely grief-stricken. Somehow the joy that we are supposed to feel serves to heighten the pain we really feel.

Mary, who comes so much to the fore at Christmas, was told very soon after Jesus' birth that a sword would pierce her soul (Luke 2:35), and so it did, as she witnessed her son crucified on a cross. The weeping of mothers like Mary, and Rachel before her, continues unabated the world over. Often it is the women who express the grief felt by all. The Coventry carol is one of the few Christmas carols to refer to the consequences of the magi's visit, and interestingly bears a notation from the late 16th century saying that this song 'the women sing'.

In the quiet, you may want to reflect on the proximity of joy and grief that is brought into the spotlight at Christmas. We are told to rejoice with those who rejoice and weep with those who weep (Romans 12:15), and that can be hard if we are experiencing the opposite emotion ourselves. Is there someone whose grief you could help to carry by sending a card or giving them a call and inviting them to have a meal with you? Or if you are the grieving one, is there someone to whom you could turn, confident that they will not shy away?

Thomas Becket

Feast day 29 December

Thomas Becket is a romantic character from the annals of English history. He was born in 1118, and, having risen through service to the Archbishop of Canterbury, was made Chancellor to King Henry II. At this stage they worked closely together and were firm friends. In 1161 the king nominated him to be the next Archbishop of Canterbury, and from this point on, there was friction between the two former allies. This resulted in Thomas going into exile, where he continued to uphold the rights of the church against the demands of the crown. After three failed attempts at mediation, Becket returned to Canterbury in 1170 in apparent triumph, but it was a fragile truce. Becket's enemies remained implacable and the king's careless words led to four knights descending on Canterbury, fully armed, where they found the archbishop in his cathedral. He was murdered by sword there beside an altar on this day, 29 December, in 1170.

Like other stories this has been romanticised and children still thrill in horror at the tale of the angry king who exclaimed, 'Will no one rid me of this turbulent priest?' Yet Thomas himself is not a wholly attractive character. Self-righteous and determined to stand on his dignity, he stubbornly refused to have any truck with his former friend. He practised his faith with deep piety but little warmth, and yet he is remembered as a saint.

The story of Becket and Henry II is about a power struggle on a public stage. To Henry, the issue was about a traitor who was questioning the rightful authority of the crown, but to Becket it was a spiritual conflict, one more incident in the eternal struggle of good and evil. That Becket was devoted to God, there can be little doubt. His austerity and severity marked him out in contrast to the lifestyle of the royal court he had previously frequented. He was not afraid to challenge his former ally, the king.

Christmas is also about power and about rulers being upset. We have already seen how Herod reacted to the perceived threat to his rule—and all from a tiny, helpless baby. As Simeon was to tell Mary, however, 'This child is destined for the falling and rising of many in Israel and to be a sign that will be spoken against' (Luke 2:34). The birth of the Christ child brought conflict in its wake because it heralded a new world order. As Isaiah had prophesied, 'Authority rests upon his shoulders' (Isaiah 9:6, NRSV).

Read and reflect on Isaiah 9:2–7.

Witnesses together in Christ

At the end of his play about Thomas Becket, *Murder in the Cathedral*, T.S. Eliot places a dialogue between three of the priests who were with Becket when he was killed. The first, in his grief, sees the church lying bereft, but another responds with the conviction that the church is stronger for its pain, fortified by persecution. Centuries ago the writer Tertullian remarked that 'the blood of the martyrs is the seed of the Church'. Today the church is suffering as much, if not more than ever before, in many parts of the world, and there are martyrdoms every day. It is going on as I write, as you read. It is difficult and painful to connect all this bloodshed with the Christmas child, until we see beneath the tinsel and perceive, if only dimly, what his birth means. The shadow of the cross overhangs the manger.

If we remember that the word 'martyr' primarily means 'witness', then the martyrs of the Church, past and present, belong with us and we belong with them. We are all members together of the body of Christ, numbered among the communion of saints. We may like to ponder, perhaps as we sit quietly by a Christmas crib or hold a favourite Christmas card in our hands, what it means to be numbered among the communion of saints and what our witness requires of us just now.

Pray for Christians everywhere to be more confident in their faith, more compassionate in their living and more creative in their mission.

St John the Evangelist

Feast day 27 December

We could refer to John as the beloved disciple. It was John who, at the last supper, lay with his head on Jesus' breast (John 13:23, KJV). He was one of the first to be called by Jesus as he mended his nets with Zebedee his father and James his brother (Mark 1:19). He was probably the only one who stood at the cross with Mary (John 19:26) and on Easter morning he went to the empty tomb with Peter and 'saw and believed' (John 20:8). Most scholars agree he wrote the fourth Gospel that bears his name. It is believed that John was the only one of the disciples to die a natural death, though he suffered for his faith, being exiled to the island of Patmos (Revelation 1:9). It is fitting that this disciple who was so close to Christ should have his feast day close to Christmas. Traditionally his Gospel is read on Christmas Day. It tells us that this same Word came and 'made his dwelling among us' (John 1:14) or, as a literal translation of the Greek word translated as 'tabernacled' would say, 'pitched his tent with us'.

Read the first letter of John, and then write your own letter to your church, imploring all to practise friendship with God, urging each one to love one another.

As John dwelt on Patmos and saw and recorded his visions of things to come, he must also have pondered the things he had witnessed and participated in. Christmas and the year's end is a good time to look back and look forward; back with thanksgiving for all that has been good, releasing the difficult things into God's keeping, and then looking forward in hope and trust. You may wish to replay some of the past year in your mind's eye, but this time in conscious awareness that you are not alone. Emmanuel is with you at each point.

When have you enjoyed the friendship of Jesus, like John? When have you run away, like John and all the others?

As you turn towards the coming year, pause at the birth of the saviour. Worship him with the shepherds and then look forward, confident that Emmanuel will walk with you every step of the way.

You might like to use 1 John 1:9 to help you as you look back and Revelation 21:1–7 as you look forward.

Darkness and light

Read John 1:4–5. Darkness and light are prominent themes at Advent and Christmas, as we welcome Jesus, the light of the world. Light and darkness are prominent themes in John's Gospel too. Darkness has figured repeatedly in these forgotten feasts that we have considered, but there has also been light, and it is important to hold fast to the confidence we have in Christ that darkness will not have the final word. The eighth-century historian and biblical scholar Bede composed a prayer that stands high above his tomb in Durham cathedral: 'Christ is the morning star, who when the light of this world is past, brings forth the light of everlasting day.'

A quotation on a prayer card (by an anonymous first-century philosopher) I carried in my purse for many years said: 'When I light a candle at midnight, I say to the darkness, I beg to differ.' You might like to light a candle in a darkened room and sit quietly with the flickering light before bringing to God situations and people who are in darkness at this time.

Passing on the good news

John the evangelist was a writer of good news. His Gospel has led millions to meet Jesus for themselves. At Christmas many churches have special services as there are visitors and there is the opportunity to explain the *evangelion*, the good news of Jesus Christ. As the poster campaign puts it, 'Christmas begins with Christ.'

You may not feel that you are a natural evangelist, but telling the story of the good news of Jesus takes many forms. You may have served in a soup kitchen, sent off a shoebox for a child somewhere you will never go, taken a neighbour to church or written a lonely person a Christmas card. Doing these things consciously in the name of Christ is part of being one of his followers. As you are asked about your Christmas and how it was, are there ways you could share something of what it really means to you? John told his story. He was in it, though he gave himself a low profile. Was that in order that his saviour should take the foreground? After all, it was God's story first and foremost. We may not all be preachers or writers, but we can all tell our stories, even if it is simply in response to the question: 'How was your day?' Taking time to reflect on our day when we are alone with God helps to raise our awareness of where he has been. Look back over the last 24 hours without judging yourself, allowing the video of the day to replay in whatever order things come. Simply focus on two questions: 'What am I thankful about today?' and 'What am I not so thankful about and what do I want to say to God about it?' Finish by asking for whatever it is you need for tomorrow.

Concluding reflections

In *Murder in the Cathedral* T.S. Eliot reminds us that it is in the realities of life, however bitter they may be, that God is at work.

The story of the martyr Stephen is found in the Acts of the Apostles, while the story of Thomas Becket is recorded in the annals of history. Acts reminds us that as followers of Jesus we, like his witnesses before us, must attend both to the words of Jesus in scripture and also to his acts, that is, the things he is doing in his church today. Christians believe that God is active in the life of his body. So we pray to be more attentive, more able to notice what he is doing and ready to join in, just as his previous witnesses were attentive and ready. To do this we must spend time with Jesus, as John the evangelist so clearly had done. Just as Stephen and Becket were called not for personal glory but for the sake of others, so are we.

'O come to us, abide with us, our Lord Emmanuel.' Meditate on these words today.

As a Child

Phil Steer

Change

> *I tell you the truth, unless you change and become like little children, you will never enter the kingdom of heaven.*
>
> MATTHEW 18:3, NIV 1984, EMPHASIS MINE

Are you one of those people who make New Year's resolutions? That moment, when the old year draws to a close and the new year stands open before us, can seem a particularly appropriate time to take stock of our lives, and resolve that things will be different from now on.

Many, feeling the effects of the festive season, resolve that they will lose weight and get fit: diet programmes are embarked upon; fitness equipment is purchased; health club membership soars. Others aim to improve their health by giving up smoking or by drinking less or by trying to reduce the stress in their lives. Some decide that they will improve their work and financial situation: by getting a better job or by saving some money or by paying off debts. Others want to expand their horizons by travelling or by learning something new; and still more resolve to spend more time with family and friends, and perhaps even find true love. For many the aim is simply to enjoy life more.

Whether or not we make New Year's resolutions, we all of us have a desire for change. Even the most contented will allow that their lives are not everything that they would want them to be—and most of us will surely accept that we are not the person that we want ourselves to be, nor the person that God wants us to be either. We know that we mess up and need to repent and receive forgiveness and allow ourselves to be transformed by God's Holy Spirit.

But how many of us have ever resolved that 'this year, I will become more like a little child'? And how many of us, when we've allowed ourselves to acknowledge the fact that we're not the person we ought to be, have recognised that our biggest need might be to become more childlike? And yet this is exactly what Jesus is saying: we need to 'change and become like little children'.

Jesus underlines the importance of his message by introducing it with the words, 'I tell you the truth.' Whenever he uses this expression, we know it is a sign that we really need to sit up and take note. What he is about to say is not simply true—after all, Jesus never spoke anything but the truth—but is a Truth, with a capital 'T'. It is something fundamental about the workings of the kingdom of heaven.

The word Jesus uses when he speaks of our need to change means 'to turn around, to change direction'. The implication is that if we are not becoming more and more childlike, then our lives are headed the wrong way. We might think that we are meant to grow up and become more adult; Jesus tells us that, on the contrary, we need in many ways to 'grow down' and become more like little children. But what might this mean?

In his parable of the sower Jesus speaks of 'the worries of this life, the deceitfulness of wealth and the desires for other things' that 'come in and choke the word [that God sows in us], making it unfruitful' (Mark 4:19). Little children do not concern themselves with such things: such worries and deceitfulness and desires. These, rather, are the attitudes and ambitions and anxieties of adulthood: 'thorns' that grow up as we grow older, entangling our heart and mind, stifling our soul and spirit, and preventing us from entering into fullness of the kingdom of heaven.

In the same way, while some might debate the extent to which little children can be said to 'sin', there can be little doubt that they succumb to very few of the temptations that so easily cause adults to stray from God's path and fall short of his standards. Writing to the churches in Galatia, Paul says, 'The acts of the sinful nature are obvious: sexual immorality, impurity and debauchery; idolatry and witchcraft; hatred, discord, jealousy, fits of rage, selfish ambition, dissensions, factions and envy; drunkenness, orgies, and the like' (Galatians 5:19–21). Look over that list again: little children just don't indulge in most of these things.

So Jesus' call for us to 'change and become like little children' must surely have something to do with a turning away from sinful thoughts and words and deeds, and from worldly cares and concerns, that we might return to the comparative innocence of childhood. And yet it means so much more than this. We are called not only to turn away from all that is wrong with our 'adult' approach to life, but also to turn towards all that is good and true in the life of a child; not only to put off our adult ways, but also to put on the ways of a child. Whenever and wherever possible, our approach to life is to be that of a little child. And this includes what we might think of as our 'spiritual life'.

We all desire to grow and mature in our faith, to enter more and more into the fullness of God's kingdom—and it's easy to believe that if only we could pray more or read our Bible more or meet more often for teaching and praise and worship, then we might begin to draw closer to God and know more of his reality in our lives. But although we might protest otherwise, this is at heart a very adult approach to God and to our faith. We are endeavouring to achieve our goal by our own efforts; trying to get what we want by doing what we think we have to do.

This is not to say that such spiritual disciplines are unnecessary or unimportant; they are, of course, God's gifts to us, which have nourished and nurtured countless Christians throughout the ages. But they are not the key to the kingdom of heaven. This, Jesus tells us, is to be found in us becoming like little children, and in coming to him as little children. All that we do in order to grow and mature in our faith must be approached in the same way, with the attitude of a little child. If not, we risk missing out on the very thing that we seek, by leaving behind the childlike faith that opens the door to God's kingdom.

Spotlight: The Scargill Community—an adventure in hospitality and prayer

Phil Stone, Director

Scargill House is idyllically set in the Yorkshire Dales. It is the home of an intentional Christian community that is both international and ecumenical. There are about 30 of us living together. In 2008, Scargill House closed and it looked as if the 50 years of ministry had come to an end. God did not think so—and with much prayer and energy, the Scargill Movement was formed with a new vision of 'Lives shared—lives transformed'. Scargill House was resurrected in early 2009. Our desire is to have Jesus at the heart of our life as we seek to be a place of hospitality and prayer; a place where people and churches can be renewed and envisioned.

The Community is intentional, and by this we mean we live by a rule of life, which we call a Pathway. Within this is a daily rhythm of prayer. The Pathway speaks about how we try our very best to 'strengthen the bonds of love' between us, how we welcome guests as if they were Jesus himself, the importance of scripture and prayer, caring for the environment, and the last promise, which is as important as the others, of 'receiving and giving unexpected treats to other people and laughing often together'. Love and laughter are part of our DNA. We should never underestimate the healing power of laughter; it isn't the poor neighbour of being serious.

Following Jesus will lead us into adventure, and people have been attracted to Scargill because they see in it an opportunity to explore active Christian faith. Oswald Sanders said, 'The frontiers of the kingdom of God were never advanced by men and women of caution' (quoted in Michael Frost and Alan Hirsch, *The Faith of Leap*, Baker Books, 2011, p. 15). All of us involved in the Scargill Movement feel that we are on an exciting adventure. *We want to join in with what God is doing*. The challenge, which takes courage, is to be continually open to the Holy Spirit, who is never predictable and full of creativity.

As well as being a place of hospitality, rest and relaxation, we offer a varied programme. We do conferences on prayer, discipleship, leadership, biblical themes; creative weeks; retreats and family holidays (particularly our SummerFest, which is an all-age arts festival in August), to mention just a few.

Places like Scargill are important to the church today because they demonstrate a different way of living. Community can be discipleship in action, an apprenticeship in following Jesus.

Learning to be a disciple...

People come to join the community for an assortment of reasons but, whatever these are, we soon find out that loving and serving one another and our guests is at the heart of our life. When I first started at Scargill, there were only about four of us, surrounded by 20,000 sheep! I felt diminished. I had been a popular vicar in London and now all there seemed to be were sheep. John 12:24 says: 'Very truly I tell you, unless a grain of wheat falls to the ground and dies, it remains only a single seed. But if it dies it produces many seeds.' Community is a place where there are many little—and some significant—deaths so that there can be new life and new beginnings.

Fragility

We soon learnt that community is a fragile enterprise. Community is not a strong place, or at least not strong in the way that the world tends to think of strength. We each bring our weaknesses as well as our strengths to communal life. As we learn to love one another, this may sometimes mean carrying each other. God does something beautiful if we allow it. Community life is not polished, not neat and tidy. For it is a place where we can dare to be truly ourselves, accepted and loved for who we are and yet also challenged to be transformed by the love of God that we experience together. Therefore the willingness to express our fragility and vulnerability is at the heart of who we are. Jesus gives us the most demanding script to play out: 'By this everyone will know that you are my disciples, if you love one another' (John 13:35).

Coming home

One of the features that distinguishes Scargill from other holiday and conference centres is that we invite people into our home and welcome them to join in our life, our rhythm of prayer and meals together. In fact, much of our rhythm is around eating and praying! Being home is an essential quality that we offer our guests. As one put it: 'Scargill is a safe place to say dangerous things.' Hospitality is about offering space for God to do his transforming work.

Sister Stan speaks of home as 'the place where we discover who we are, where we are coming from and where we are going to. It is where we are helped to establish our own identity. It is where we learn to love and be loved' (Sister Stanislaus Kennedy, *Gardening the Soul: a spiritual daybook through the seasons*, TownHouse, 2001, entry for 25 December).

Intentional community can be a very rich experience and Scargill is a place of love and laughter, challenge and tears, hospitality and welcome. A place where hearts and minds are expanded. A place where I can learn to be an authentic follower of Jesus.

To find out more about the Scargill Movement, please email admin@scargillmovement.org, ring Phil Stone on 01756 761236, or go to the website at www.scargillmovement.org.

Quiet Spaces Subscription

Please note one-year subscription prices below include postage and packing.

You can also purchase your subcription by Direct Debit. Complete the details on the direct debit form and post to BRF with the order form.

Please send *Quiet Spaces* beginning with the January 2015/May 2015/ September 2015 issue (delete as applicable).

PRICES FOR UK ADDRESSES

DESCRIPTION	PRICE	QUANTITY ORDERED	TOTAL
Individual 1-year subscription includes postage and packing	£15.99		
Group 1-year subscription postage and packing FREE	£12.75		
ORDER TOTAL			

PRICES FOR OVERSEAS ADDRESSES

DESCRIPTION	PRICE	QUANTITY ORDERED	TOTAL
Individual 1-year subscription Airmail includes postage and packing	£25.50		
Individual 1-year subscription Surface includes postage and packing	£23.25		
ORDER TOTAL			

Prices are correct at time of going to press and subject to change.
For information about group subscriptions, see overleaf or contact BRF at the address given on the next page.

Promo code: QS0314

Method of payment

☐ Cheque ☐ MasterCard ☐ Maestro ☐ Visa ☐ Postal Order

Card no. ☐☐☐☐ ☐☐☐☐ ☐☐☐☐ ☐☐☐☐ ☐☐

Shaded boxes for Maestro use only

Valid from ☐☐☐☐ Expires ☐☐☐☐ Issue No. (Switch only) ☐☐☐☐

Security code* ☐☐☐ (Last 3 digits on the reverse of the card / *Essential in order to process your order*) *0000* **000** EXAMPLE

Signature .... Date ..../..../....

All subscription orders must be accompanied by the appropriate payment.
Please note: do not send payments for group orders. All group orders will be invoiced.

Name ....

Acc. No. ....

Address..

.... Postcode ....

Telephone..

Email..

If you and a minimum of four friends subscribe to *Quiet Spaces* or BRF's other Bible reading notes (*New Daylight, Day by Day with God, Guidelines, The Upper Room*), you can form a group. What's so good about being in a group? You pay the price of the notes only—postage is free for delivery to a UK address. (All notes are sent to one address.) All group orders are invoiced. No advance payment is required. For more information, see www.biblereadingnotes.org.uk/group-subscriptions/ or contact the BRF office.

BRF, 15 The Chambers, Vineyard, Abingdon OX14 3FE;
Tel: 01865 319700   Fax: 01865 319701
www.brf.org.uk   email: enquiries@brf.org.uk
BRF is a Registered Charity (no: 233280)

BRF Quiet Days

BRF Quiet Days are an ideal way of redressing the balance in our busy lives. Held in peaceful locations around the country, each one is led by an experienced speaker and gives the opportunity to reflect, be silent and pray, and through it all to draw closer to God.

Friday 3 October: 'Matthew: his Master's Voice' led by David Winter at Douai Abbey, Upper Woolhampton, Reading, Berkshire, RG7 5TQ

Thursday 27 November: 'Ray of Light: a quiet day for Advent' led by Ian Adams at Mill House, Rochnell Manor Farm, Westleigh, Tiverton, Devon, EX16 7ES

Monday 1 December: 'Mary' led by Andrew Jones at Gladstone's Library, Church Lane, Hawarden, Flintshire, CH5 3DF

For further details and to book, please go to www.brfonline.org.uk/events-and-quiet-days or contact us at BRF, 15 The Chambers, Vineyard, Abingdon, Oxfordshire, OX14 3FE; tel: 01865 319700

Direct Debit

You can pay for your annual subscription to BRF notes using Direct Debit. You need to give your bank details only once, and the payment is made automatically every year until you cancel it. If you would like to pay by Direct Debit, please use the form opposite, entering your BRF account number under 'Reference'.

You are fully covered by the Direct Debit Guarantee:

The Direct Debit Guarantee

- This Guarantee is offered by all banks and building societies that accept instructions to pay Direct Debits.
- If there are any changes to the amount, date or frequency of your Direct Debit, The Bible Reading Fellowship will notify you 10 working days in advance of your account being debited or as otherwise agreed. If you request The Bible Reading Fellowship to collect a payment, confirmation of the amount and date will be given to you at the time of the request.
- If an error is made in the payment of your Direct Debit, by The Bible Reading Fellowship or your bank or building society, you are entitled to a full and immediate refund of the amount paid from your bank or building society.
  - If you receive a refund you are not entitled to, you must pay it back when The Bible Reading Fellowship asks you to.
- You can cancel a Direct Debit at any time by simply contacting your bank or building society. Written confirmation may be required. Please also notify us.

The Bible Reading Fellowship

Instruction to your bank or building society to pay by Direct Debit

Please fill in the whole form using a ballpoint pen and send to The Bible Reading Fellowship, 15 The Chambers, Vineyard, Abingdon OX14 3FE.

Service User Number: | 5 | 5 | 8 | 2 | 2 | 9 |

Name and full postal address of your bank or building society

| To: The Manager .... |
| .... Bank/Building Society |
| Address .... |
| .... |
| .... Postcode .... |

Name(s) of account holder(s)

Branch sort code

☐☐ – ☐☐ – ☐☐

Bank/Building Society account no.

☐☐☐☐☐☐☐☐

Reference

☐☐☐☐☐☐☐

Instruction to your Bank/Building Society

Please pay The Bible Reading Fellowship Direct Debits from the account detailed in this instruction, subject to the safeguards assured by the Direct Debit Guarantee. I understand that this instruction may remain with The Bible Reading Fellowship and, if so, details will be passed electronically to my bank/building society.

| Signature(s) |
| .... |
| Date |

Banks and Building Societies may not accept Direct Debit instructions for some types of account.